The Age of Change

A Challenging Path to the Future

The Age of Change

A Challenging Path to the Future

Printed in the United States of America
Published by Quintessence
First Printing January 2017

www.OnereonChannels.com

Cover Image - Andrey Prokhorov/Shutterstock

ISBN # 978-0-9969371-3-9

"We that change, hate change. We that pass, love what abides." D. T. Suzuki

"I cannot say whether things will get better if we change; what I can say is they must change if they are to get better." Georg C. Lichtenberg

"You never change things by fighting the existing reality. To change something, build a new model that makes the existing model obsolete." R. Buckminster Fuller

The Age of Change

ARE YOU AFRAID? It may appear that we are living through fearful times. Fear does not exist from some outside source but rather from the inner energy of each individual human. In a great sense, it is a choice of every being to live in fear or make a different decision. The energy of fear arrives as a reaction to the energy of change and shifting reality.

This, then, is the true age we exist in—not one of fear, but one of great change and shifting. The alternate choice to feeling fear is to feel excitement and enthusiasm. Appreciate that not all things remain constant, and the best way to gain a bright future is to go with the flow of natural energies, which frees us from the need to grasp at what is old energy or philosophy. It allows us to exist with eyes forward, looking to the future instead of to regret and longing for the past.

The past has passed. The present moment is the point of choice. It is where you live now. The future is where you are going, and this brings with it new ways of living. Attempting to drag old ways into new realities never works. Why clutter up the future? Why darken the day ahead with the pain of yesterday? Release such old energy, and rejoice that the new day offers opportunities for you to be better in many ways.

Of course, not all things need to shift or change. But points of imbalance, anger, or resentment—anything that causes division or creates unnecessary gaps between living beings—are the things that can readily be released and sent away to the past. Progress, harmony, and discovery— anything that allows for beings to come together and enter the future with joy and peace emanating from within, from their primal karmic entities—are the powerful things that create positive futures.

It is not as simple as one or two beings shifting their personal perspectives, however. There are those who seek to harm others, to hold them back and destroy their vision of change. Why? Because they themselves fear change at their deepest core level of physical existence. They cannot or will not see the universe as abundant, and they seek to acquire for themselves the bulk of supplies. They seek to control and dominate the flow of energy that should and could be free for all beings. A cooperative society with an eye to distributing basic needs to all beings is possible, but the majority of beings must be vigilant, watching for greed pools and stagnation of power.

The current of time naturally wears away institutions that attempt to establish themselves as rocklike and unchanging. It takes time—years, sometimes decades. In certain monolithic traditions it could take centuries, but even then these things alter internally until they break apart or reconfigure into something with meaning for a modern society.

What we see today is a vast array of information and a growing phalanx of humanity who no longer find value in old and outmoded traditions. These generations, with clarity of logic and transparency of the motives of those in power, are unable to understand why such traditions existed. In time, these ones and their children will simply ignore archaic philosophies, and the structure of these obsolete ways will collapse. Until then, there are many who remain attached to the past and seek to shape the future to look like what was and never will be again.

It is important to comprehend that you can only change one person on the planet, yourself. You are not an agent of karma. But in this, understand also that no one can truly change or alter your karmic core.

Be who you are now, and allow all else to slip into history. Grow toward light, and leave shadows behind.

Humanity knows too much to ever willingly return to ignorance and superstition. We are losing our capacity for fear and discovering our joy and enthusiasm for the future. What is next? It depends on how you view the future.

An Introduction to
The Onereon Channels

ONEREON IS A GROUP OF BEINGS that define themselves as "together." They indicate that, during channeling, anyone that is in the room is potentially a member of the group Onereon and thus "together." This will hold equally true for any who are readers of these pages. They describe this togetherness not necessarily as an agreement, but rather as a direction of energy; together in purpose.

Onereon currently comes through to me in three main personalities, each distinct but separate and having definite points of view. I often describe them as "Human Resources," as if we are all working for a cosmic company and exist in different departments. There are others in the department as well; they just do not seem to come through as often.

There is a great deal of humor and compassion that comes through during the channeling sessions. When reading the transcriptions, be aware of the wryness and sometimes ironic tone that the communications contain. There is always underlying warmth to their comments that I find comforting and invigorating.

Above all else, the Onereon group believes in us and our ability to grow and evolve. Much of what they say is indicative of the future of humanity and the vitality of the planetary system that we are a part of, Gaia and her companion.

They point out that we are not as important as individuals but, as energetic beings that have existed essentially forever, we are, in fact, aspects of Source, the singular energy of creation. Whatever form we take is an equally important expression of creation. They also point out that we are not the pinnacle of creation.

For some this may seem disappointing. Onereon also points out that they themselves are not the pinnacle of creation. They are also quick to include themselves in the "not as important" category. The phrase we use to open the channeling sessions, "As above, so below," has an equal application to them in the realm of spirit as it does to us in the realm of physicality.

Frequent references to the idea of body, mind, and spirit punctuate the channels, helping us to understand the need to stay grounded in the physical world while we pursue our spiritual pathways and goals.

Of the word "mind" that is used in the phrase "body, mind, and spirit," Onereon is quick to indicate that it is not simply the way we think or the use of our intellectual capacities, but the balance of emotional energies of the heart with the logic energies of the brain. Thus the term "mind" takes on the meaning of heart and brain working together. Spirit, they say, cannot be comprehended by logic, but only by emotion. Still, spirit is ultimately logical.

Onereon also speaks of us as energetic beings in the same way that we can describe water. Once we change, as in birth or death, we are not the same personality. We recombine and become different than we were, in the same way as a drop of water goes into a pool and joins together its molecules with other water molecules. The chances then of the individual molecules all forming together into the exact same drop are extremely slim. In this same way, we do not come back to the earth repeatedly as the same personality. We do remain life energy, however, and sometimes we are physical and sometimes we are in spirit form. The reasons for this are explained through the channels.

There is a change coming in the way that we will all communicate. Onereon indicates that this change has been going on for about two hundred years and will continue another one hundred or so. They point out that our way of communicating has already changed and continues to change dramatically in the physical realm. "So below" they say, then also "as above." In other words, look at how fast we now communicate with each other on the planet and you will have a clue about how fast we will communicate with those in the spirit realm in the future.

Onereon reminds us that we, as a human species, have reached a level of maturity where we must now take responsibility for our lives and our future. The time for continually calling on spirit as guides or angels, to grant us some favor or blessing, is soon to pass. We are capable of doing many of these things ourselves, of creating what we choose for our life on the planet. They encourage us to see them more as companions, fellow spiritual seekers and partners in the enjoyment of all creation on all levels.

Onereon indicates that this is a returning to a way of life, one in which spirit and body are not separated but joined together with a balanced mind, acting in concert and growth towards a peaceful future, not just for life on Earth but throughout the Universe in all its forms.

I am happy to have been chosen as the voice of this warm, wise, and witty group and am pleased to be able to present to you this information as I am allowed to perceive it.

Entries may have been edited for better understanding in the written form, otherwise the content remains uniquely their own.

Jeff Michaels

The name Onereon is pronounced
O nair ee on

Table of Contents

1
Coming Together

AS ABOVE, SO BELOW.

That phrase, our opening phrase, will lose some of its meaning as the illusion of distance closes between those of us in the spirit realm and those of you here on planet Earth. There are other places in the Universe where "as above, so below" is a phrase that would not be understood, for there is no distinct separation of physical beings from the spiritual realm.

There are areas of the Universe that are consistently enjoying love and joy and peace. The planet Earth will soon be one of those areas. This time is approaching more rapidly than you might imagine if you are observing world events.

Those with spiritual vision and discernment see more clearly how the physical realm and the realm of spiritual beings are becoming more unified. But for you here now, today, understand that there is still a separation. It is closing. We are getting closer. We continually get closer, and that is because of you and your work in the physical realm.

An Age of Change

The twentieth century and the early part of the twenty-first century, how remarkable! Think of the changes. Think of the things that you have gone through. Think about one hundred years ago, and imagine taking someone from then and bringing him or her to the present day. What would this person understand? What would this person know? Yet you take it all in stride. Now imagine that someone from one hundred years from now approaches you and shows you his or her world. What will you understand of that life?

As your technology increases, improves, and flourishes, you have a hint of what is returning to the family human in the way of abilities. These days, you can talk to anyone anywhere in the world with a small box that fits in your pocket. Now imagine this: talking to anyone, anywhere in the world, without any technology. You can imagine it, but you cannot yet do it. Your vibration has not risen to that point. You are getting there. You feel it. You sense it. You know it.

For your children, use of the current technology is normal to them. And as for their children, have you ever seen toddlers with a smartphone? They know how to use it! How did that happen? When they were above in the realm of spirit, they were guides. They knew what kind of world they wanted to be born into, and they know what kind of a world they want to leave when the time comes.

In your society, restrictive coils are unwinding. They are loosening. Think about gender issues, various forms of pairing and bonding and mating; the boundaries are now dissolving around the world. How quickly they have been shifting, and it took a long time for that wave to crest, did it not? Once the wave breaks, all the old prejudices and bigotries just fade away, do they not? They just cannot exist. Restrictive social energy is unwinding. We have long spoken of the societal and spiritual differences you will see on the planet in one hundred years, becoming unrecognizable to someone alive during the twentieth century. The humans living on Earth one hundred years from now will not be able to comprehend the artificial divisions that have existed in society for so long.

Waves of changing energy happen first in the spirit world. Then they move into one's heart, and you know this. Then they move on to the intellect, and you know this. Finally, change begins happening on the physical level. Many hearts and intellects are being opened to receive these waves of change from the realm of spirit. There is much more that is going to happen—much more unwinding, much more loosening. You will live to see some of it. In the unwinding, many things will shake loose and separate. Many things will sink back to Earth to be recycled, to be repurposed.

What you on the planet have been enduring—the tensions, the fierceness of the world—is all shaking loose. The tensions are unraveling. It could take some time. There will be equal and opposite reactions against these shifts. Still. Yet.

In the Universe, we in the spirit realm see all of this from above. We see this with a higher perspective. Where you are—so below—in gravity (where the physical manifestation happens last) shifts can appear to occur quickly in certain situations. Do not despair if it seems that there is a retrograde of progressive concepts. Old beliefs have deep roots, but their soil is shallow. Winds of change are toppling them.

The New Normal

The Universe does not support conformity; it only supports diversity. You in the metaphysical and spiritual society have been on the far edge of diversity in human society. You have appeared to be odd and out of step with the old norms of religious dogma. Understand that what is odd in the past is now becoming the new normal. Accept that role. Accept it. Revel in it. Love it. Make fun of yourselves. Do not take yourselves too seriously. It does not pay. It becomes too heavy. Vibrations slow down in heaviness, becoming lower.

You are on the planet now. Enjoy it. Look around for ways that you think the world can improve. When you are "as above," you get to handle some of those projects. We are looking forward to it. We, now "as above," will then be here where you are, "so below."

As Onereon, we say, "We are together." We are together in purpose. However, we all speak in our unique voices, do we not? Who do you think we are? Would you like to see us? Would you like to see what we look like?

Turn to your left. Turn to your right. Look into the eyes of the people next to you. Please, look into the eyes of the people next to you right now. Look at them. Say, "I see you." [Audience interacts.] And so you see us, for we are you and you are us!

There are lofty beings being channeled here today [at the Kryon Summer Light Conference in Sedona], and we are humbled—not by these lofty beings, but by you. Many, above in the realm of spirit, are preparing now to be reincarnated below. You have their gratitude because you are making this planet better.

Every one of the channels here today is affected by your gratitude. These channels are quite used to being with higher-vibrational beings, spirit beings responsible for guiding great energies, yet it is you here in the physical realm who affect us with your gratitude. Imagine, then, if your gratitude reaches beyond the physical realm, what powerful results it is creating within that same physical realm.

Your gratitude, your higher vibration, and your spiritual nature—what is happening to the world as you radiate those energies outward? We want you to think about that now because the love that Source is, is in you, and it is powerful. Things get in the way of it, don't they? Things slow your love down. Things get in the way of you radiating your light. But do not stop radiating your light!

Imagine that your heart is a source of visible light. Image that right now. That light would not just shine straight out of your chest. It shines in every direction and on everyone. Imagine that your heart radiates love. Do that now. Do that tomorrow. Do that in a month. Consciously radiate love out of your heart in all directions. When you are with others, radiate love. Even when you are in the company of difficult people. Life is unpredictable. You never know when it will be the last time they will be able to feel love here on planet Earth. Until the next time, of course. And there is always the next time. We promise.

So you are love. Do you want to know who we are? We are you. Do you want to be closer to us? Do you want to feel us closer to you? Begin to imagine us less as guides, less as angels, and less as beings who need to be bowed down to. Imagine us more as companions, more like those people who are sitting next to you right now, because we are next to you. And you are next to us. In this, you assist in closing the distance between the realm of spirit and the physical realm of Earth.

You have the gratitude of the beings in heaven. You have our love, and you are loved. Live in peace. Practice peace. Pursue peace. Seek peace. Enjoy this life. This world is beautiful. Please keep that in your minds and in your hearts. It is a good planet to be on.

2
Who Do You Think You Are?

AS ABOVE, SO BELOW. We have a question for you: Who do you think you are? Do you think you are physical bodies? You are not *just* physical bodies, but you *are* physical bodies. You have to acknowledge and respect that. These bodies move you around the planet. These bodies touch and taste and see and feel and hear. These bodies give you experiences on the planet. There is a reason for this.

It is a good planet to be on, isn't it? You are here on the planet to experience things in a very specific way. As above, we do not experience things in the same manner. As above, we have a higher vibrational perspective that you do not have. Imagine that we are on a mountain and you are in a valley. We will see many things that you cannot. On the planet, you experience many things in ways we cannot.

You are spiritual beings having a physical experience. Source at one point was one big ball of energy, and it said, "I want to be different," so it diversified. You are all diverse, and you are all experiencing this amazing planet in various ways. We, Onereon, have been incarnate on the planet, and we enjoyed it. You have been dis-incarnate in the realm of spirit. Do you remember? You will be again.

At some point, you will not be a physical being. Some of you have been doing this work for a very, very long time. Maybe the term "new age" was new when you started out, and now you are more "old age." So those old-age New Agers are going to be moving along, and we are here to help with that. People fear that transition. "What if no one remembers me? What if I do not finish my song? What if I do not finish _____?" Finish what? Finish having experiences? Finish having love?

We want you to be joyful at the end of life. We want you to say, "This is great. I cannot wait to see what is next!" We want you to have a pleasant passing. Do not cling to this gravity. Move on because there are other things coming. There are new things coming. In one hundred years, this world will not be recognizable as what it is today. This is much the same for one hundred years ago, right? Except this coming change will be more of a social and psychological nature. Fewer humans will be on the planet at that time, but those here will be humans of a higher vibrational nature.

You are giving birth to them. You are teaching them. Your children are giving birth to higher vibrational beings. It is their children who are really going to take a hold of this planet. They are really going to start to listen to the planet and release the potential for the planet to do what it wants to do. They will not try to own it, control it, or change it. Rather, they will live in harmony with Gaia, the living planet who also is a spiritual being, who also is ascending in a higher vibrational way.

You Are Energy

Everybody here knows that everything is energy. You are energy. You are pure energy, and you happen to have come together, coalesced into a very specific physical form. You are an aspect, a particle, of the Source—the energy that created everything. You are connected to that. Who do you think you are? Do you think you are just these little bodies? When you transform out of this body— and you will—please remember: Energy cannot be created or destroyed; it can only be transformed. And you are energy.

When your physical life concludes, suddenly you are on the other side of the veil, and it is not as you might have been taught. There are no angels playing harps on clouds. When you arrive in the spiritual realm, you are going to have tasks to accomplish because you are doing good work here. And the reward for good work is what? More work! We in the spirit realm have responsibilities. We need your help. Please. We are not trying to rush you. Come when you are ready. Come naturally. You will be greeted warmly.

You have heard about the tunnel of light in near-death experiences. That is just the beginning. Your energy transfers from the physical realm, and you are greeted by kind of a reverse hospice. Hospice helps you transform out of this life. Reverse hospice helps you transform back into spirit nature. The first thing that happens is the wash of love. We love you until all those things that weighed you down, all the remnants of gravity—the pains, the hurts, the fears, the betrayals, the disappointments, the loss, the sense of confusion that you feel—are gone. This is the wash of love. All sentient beings pass through this phase.

Then we put you to work! Sometimes you go back to what you were doing before. Sometimes it is an echo of what you were doing on the planet. Sometimes it is something completely different. We want to be sure that you are working at your highest potential for joy and happiness. If you have raised your vibration while living on Earth, you will experience a rise in your level of responsibility as well.

We Are All Here Together in Purpose

We in the spirit realm want to be close to you. We want you to know us well. We want you to communicate with us. We want you to communicate freely. We want it to be less "as above, so below" and more "we are all here together." That is what the term "Onereon" means—together. It does not necessarily mean together in agreement but rather together in purpose—together as people seeking peace, together as spiritual seekers.

We want interaction to happen easily because when you transform, it is our time to come back to the physical realm. "As above" becomes you, and "so below" becomes us. When we are in physical form, we want to have a good connection. We want it to be natural. We want it to be close so that when we are on the planet talking to you in the spiritual realm, you are able to respond easily.

We know it is going to be tough when we are back on the planet. There will be messes to clean up. Yes, it is getting better, but it is going to be hard work. There is a deconstruction going on, and the old, dogmatic energy is holding on and trying to pull things back.

Fundamentalism is working very hard to restructure you so that you fit into an old box, and you do not want to go there, do you? No, because you are spiritual and you cannot put spirit into a box no matter how hard you try. You are already a mature spiritual being, currently on the planet in a physical form. All you need to do is get off the planet to act directly in a spiritual way, unimpeded by gravity.

Act in Peace, Love, and Joy

The quality of humanity on the planet will increase. It will be better. Your children's children and their children, they are already preparing. Those karmic entities are already lining up. They are already asking, "Where is our energy going to be needed the most? What is the most challenging thing we can do?" They are lining up. They are coalescing. They will be very interesting humans, like those we have not seen in recorded history. We give you a hint there: "recorded history." There have been other humans on this planet. They left no trace because they cooperated with Gaia. We will renew that cooperative attitude.

You are going to do it. You will start from "above" and then come back to "below." As the cycle of incarnation continues, it is going to be easier for all of us in so many ways. The pressure will be off. You will return to a planet that is already purified to a great extent. It will be a time of growth, rebirth, beauty, and light. Can you see this?

What do you need to do now? Remember these three things:

- Act peacefully. It is vital. Find peace within yourself.

- Act in love. That is sometimes the difficult one. Start with the people who are easy to love. Start with yourself. Please, love yourself.

- Act in joy. Enjoy yourselves. Find what gives you joy. Find what gives you pleasure. Enjoy yourself as you are, and understand who you are, who you have been, and who you can become through the paths of love and joy and peace.

Thank you very much for sharing time with us today. It is a beautiful world, and you make it more beautiful.

3

Spiritual Growth in Uncertain Times

AS ABOVE, SO BELOW. It is said that the only constant in the Universe is the energy of change. For many, this is a difficult thing to deal with. The desire for certainty is linked with the search for safety and comfort. The energy of change is such that it makes life uncertain. There is a wide spectrum of change and most often those alive on planet Earth exist somewhere in the middle range. However, there are times when this energy of change is at a peak. We are in this stage now.

The state of uncertainty that the world exists in now is steep. That energy of change is flowing rapidly, like water down a hill. It cannot be contained. It cannot be stopped. However, it can be channeled. It can be useful. To do so, beings must leave their zones of comfort and accept the idea of change. They must form their own channels or paths to create results they desire.

From our place in the spirit realm, we see how the majority of humanity has not set up channels to contain and to manipulate the energy. This causes confusion and, oftentimes, fear.

Confusion is based on perception—what you thought was true or certain proves to be elusive or lacking a basis in reality. Confusion is based on looking down rather than up. Looking down to make sure that we do not stumble, we fail to look up to see where we are heading. There is a balance to be attained, and the more certain you are of your own abilities to walk your path, the more time you can spend in perceiving the options and opportunities available to you. Much energy is drawing people's vision downward. There is much talk that is fear-based. This is a trap for much of humanity. It is a trap humanity sets for itself.

Escaping the Trap of Fear

Being in the physical realm, there will be an instinct to either flee a fearful situation or to turn and do battle. These reactions are not inherently wrong. However, they are physically rather than spiritually based. If you find yourself in the energy of fear, you can view it as an opportunity. Image a different outcome, image the veil, image the idea that you are a higher being, and then look down on what you are fearing, making it smaller by perception. Things become easier to handle now.

It is said in the larger patterns of existence that there is no right or wrong; there is only the present moment. By remaining centered or balanced, beings can look ahead from where they stand and chart their course in a spiritually conscious manner.

Time passing shows that many of the things that are feared in the present moment were not fearful at all in the context of history. Yet in the present day, an increasing number of people feel the need to fear. It is the only emotion that they feel comfortable with.

Your existence continues. Whether you live in fear or whether you seek to live in love while alive in the physical realm is a matter of choice; it is a matter of balance. We see the world struggling to live in fear. This is a choice that, in many ways, is being forced on the world by lower-vibrational beings currently coexisting on the planet.

The reason there is a base of cooperation with this fear within human consciousness at the moment is because so many have come back from similar situations in previous incarnations where they were in fear, where they perished or were injured to the point of mortality, and where their lives were taken away from them beyond their control. So this echo, this pattern, this ripple, continues. All humanity is being offered a choice to shed this energy. For many, this is difficult.

The Opportunity for Peace

Many have heard the concept or express a desire for the world to enter a peaceful era. Could this happen? The answer is yes. That era will primarily be the result of things being done in the spiritual realm. It will also be the result of Earth and the solar system moving through space to a place of calm, away from seemingly undetectable rough energies. These rough energies are detectable; it is just not known how to look for them.

The rough passage is nearing conclusion. There may be some of your generation, those of full maturity, who see the beginnings of this. But for the most part, the generation of humans being born now will witness it fully. They will see life in general in a very different way. The passing of the fear-based generations is in progress. Then after the passing of the self-based generations, we enter into an experience of potential—of generations who wonder "what if?" before they ask "why?"

The question is asked, *"Can you give an example of any humans channeling the energy we are dealing with on the planet at this time toward 'positive' growth-oriented directions?"*

Many seek to accomplish the task of overcoming fear-based existence. It is often single, anonymous people rather than organized groups. We will say that, generally speaking, political leaders are not amongst them after they reach a certain level of power. Religious leaders also are not amongst them after they reach a certain level of hierarchy. These people might begin their course with good intentions, and they could set certain channels for the energy of change to flow. Soon, however, they run into other people's channels of energy. So there is a mingling of their energy with other energies, and what might have begun as a pure path becomes entangled.

Strong leaders can maintain their personal balance. One might admire the current pope, yet his channels, his intentions, must combine with the other leaders of this ancient and entrenched organization. He could choose to try to channel energy in a particular way. As a being with less responsibility, this was easier to do. Now, as he holds more responsibility, he must struggle to get others to align with him and to understand that he faces an energetic countercurrent.

In his instance, he is a being who has a true higher-vibrational quality and must deal with intensely low-vibrational matters as he struggles to alter a perception. From a purely physical standpoint, it may appear that his efforts will fail. Yet it is not the outcome as much as the energy he puts forth. It is not so much the completion; it is more the "try"—the effort of seeking the balance—that sets the stage for future balance, that sets the example for future energetic beings to ponder and to ask the question, "Well, if this can be changed, then why or why not shift opinion or perception in other ways?" He sets the stage for possibility thinking.

What the current and past generations do best is ask the question, "Why?" Understand that we are now energetically moving away from that question and into the "What if?" area of generated energies. This means society—the structure, the base appearance of physical life—must change before the "what if?" questions can be asked in a more powerful manner. The energy of "why?" exists strongly, and it has served humanity well. It now needs to be reduced. The many channels of "why?" need to be pulled back in so that when the channels of "what if?" begin, they will flow freely, opening up in a strong passage to peaceful coexistence, and they will. And they will. They will.

For now, you can see that what started out as a question that opened energy and moved things forward—the word "why": "why 'this'?" or "why 'that'?"—brought human society up and out of what is called the darkened age to enlightenment. The more questions that were asked, the more answers became available. Less superstition existed and more reality of the physical realm returned to be available to human consciousness.

The energy of that unenlightened time is now distant. As new life is now being brought to the planet, it heralds the birth of a new wave of existence. We are in the beginning stage of such a new phase. Karmic entities are being prepared for this before they return to life in the physical realm.

It is a time of balancing. It is an adaptation of perceptions. In that, adaptation is the evolution of all things toward peaceful coexistence. Seek to radiate peaceful energy. Bring your vitality to the highest perception you possibly can reach in each life. Dispel fear with love and joy. Spiral forward. Seek the future and, as your energy transfers away from this planet, smile, because you too are about to enter a new phase and attain a new energetic life.

We will conclude our session here as we always do, emphasizing the words "love" and "joy" and "peace," because these are the most powerful nature-based energies available to you from Source. It is natural for Source to seek balance through the action of love. All energies balance through the action of the spiral. It is that pattern that we work within in the realm of spiritual nature. Image the spiral as well as those energies of love and joy and peace.

4

Pursuing True Spirituality through Courage and Imagination

As ABOVE, SO BELOW. You have entered a great era of shift and change. The promise of the future is powerful and fine. The path to achieve such a new golden age is difficult and not always clear.

You, the humans alive today, face more new realities than ever before. Do you feel the stress of simple day-to-day living? It is not imagined. You are not weak.

The times ahead are ones that require strenuous activity on the part of each being who seeks to raise the vibration of the community of Gaia. The search for true spirituality and balance of energy is what is behind much of the struggle that you witness within global society today.

What steps, then, what specific areas of action, will be the most beneficial to take? What is your best personal course? True spirituality is a difficult thing to realize in stressful times. Remember that gold is purified in fire.

Act from Your Heart

The very first step to practice is courage. When we use this term, our meaning is applied to the energetic heart of the individual human. The heart is the point where the physical human most easily connects to the spiritual realm. It is there that you are able to most purely sense and share the powerful energy of Source that is commonly called love. Hence, for our purposes, the quality of courage connects directly to the energy of love.

Courage is not about being brave in a battle though it is often evident in such a scenario. Courage is the quality of acting from your heart, being true to your own sense of love and your personal vision of true spirituality. In being courageous, the member of the family human will leave behind all that is not love. They will seek to act in accord with others even when there is not a shared cultural belief. In doing so, the spiritual seeker will transcend the imagined need for maintaining the old structures and archaic philosophies of the past. The requirement for courage in this age is to simply refuse to follow old patterns and concepts that lead to old arguments and wars. These are not things that need to be taught nor are the battles necessary to be fought.

Imagine the Future

Ponder what life will be like when the old enmities and religions have faded to allow the light of the true nature of spirituality to shine out from every being. Keep close in your thoughts the very clear concepts of how the family human desires peace and security. Bring into your consciousness the more beautiful principles that can be chosen by people of Earth. Image growth, health, abundance, community, and the passing of new wisdom to the coming generations.

These are pleasant things to consider, yet many find this difficult to do. Why? It is because of the overbearing amount of information that passes unbidden into your eyes and ears throughout your daily existence. There is constant chattering of what many feel is important news and information. You as a human are inundated with data that does not serve you in any way. Much of this so-called news is truly worthless. Much of it is simply untrue. Yet with repetition, you will find that many become weak in their ability to discern reality from fiction. Many take up the worthless chatter and repeat it verbatim with little or no critical thought. They do not examine the information to ascertain its worth. In doing so, they lessen their power and individuality. They themselves lessen their worth to the planet.

It may seem a simple matter to redirect your attention away from such noise, yet there is an addictive quality to this constant data stream. It gives one a false sense of self-importance, as if knowing many bits of information somehow completes you.

Ask yourself now: are the images presented to me through media representative of the world I wish to live in or pass on to the next generations? Or do they cause me unnecessary distress? Breaking the trend to be connected to the world through such communication can be easy. It requires the aforementioned quality of courage. It is merely a matter of each individual speaking a new thought, one that does not carry the sense of fear or judgment. In your connections to your own community, do not respond to ones who promote fear or anger. Rather, consciously reflect the concepts of true spirituality in every sentence you create.

This requires critical thinking on the part of the individual. It is not something that society is currently training anyone to actively pursue. You must motivate yourself from your heart and its connection to spirit, true spirituality. It is not a single step to that goal but many steps, and the journey is long. Many are taking these steps today. The result will be powerful in the future. Acting in this manner now will begin to benefit you, the individual, in subtle ways. Raising the vibration of the family human is a process, not an event.

Achieving True Spirituality

Engaging these two qualities—courage and imagination—will unite the energies of the heart and the brain. It is this combination that creates what we call the mind, and it is this that completes the individual when we refer to the body, the mind, and the spirit. All humanity is possessed of such a combination. Yet not all are balanced in these qualities. Strengthening the mind is vital to achieving true spirituality in your life. It is also vital to attaining a strong physical presence on Earth. There is no separation of these three elements, and each is interconnected. When you strengthen and purify one, the others become more active and healthy. Balanced humans raise their personal vibrations. This, then, radiates outward and creates a balancing effect on their community.

True spirituality is powerful. It requires courage and imagination. A being who is truly acting from spirit will release the need for judgment. They will seek to pass along wisdom, not through any insistence on a specific teaching, but rather through the example of their own lives. Their actions will speak for them.

Spiritual beings will not have the need for outside validation. They will not feel the need to conform to old tribal pressures. They will act from the energetic state of love. Their goal will surely be peace, but they will not use force to impose their will on others.

Humans who pursue true spirituality will fully comprehend the power of happiness and will thus seek to create such a world through their words and activities. They will understand that happiness is a choice and gladly make that choice for themselves no matter the economic or societal conditions they find themselves living in. That choice is not always an easy one. There is much that can leach away the energy of happiness. However, by acting and striving toward such a life-nurturing quality, beings will find themselves gaining companions who seek the same joyful outlook in their lives.

Gaining a balance of the body, mind, and spirit is a challenge in this day and age. It can be done, but as we have stated, it is a path to walk, not an event to attend. The old systems are fading. Their roots are withering, and they bear fruit that is bitter to the world. Yet some continue to seek to support and grow such dying ideologies. It is only by creating new, healthy, and vital communities that the family human can—and will—turn from the past and begin to craft the future. Each being who seeks and practices the concepts of true spiritual living helps the global community take another step toward that future—a time of happiness, diversity, creativity, and wonder.

The path is there. It is sometimes crowded. It is sometimes lonely. It is often strewn with obstacles. Often these obstacles are mere perceptions, reflections of past fears. By looking forward with spiritual vision based in the qualities of love, joy, and peace, these obstacles fade, and the path widens and clears.

Recall always that you are crafted from the elements of the physical body present on the planet; the mind, which is the heart and brain acting in concert; and spirit, that aspect of your awareness that senses and supports the connection to the Source energy of the Universe in which you dwell. Peace arrives through your physical nature. Joy arrives through the strength of the heart and support from the brain. Love arrives from the realm of spirit.

Against these things, there is no law.

5
Gaia's Communication

AS ABOVE, SO BELOW. Our opening statement carries many levels of meaning. We speak of the spiritual realm being, in essence, the same as the physical realm. We draw your attention to this concept in an effort to demonstrate a fuller reality available to the seeker of a higher vibrational life. There is a deep interconnectedness of thought and emotion represented here.

All life is intertwined. This may seem an obvious statement to some, but our meaning is deeper than simply understanding the nature of the physical ecosystem. In the same way that a member of the family human is comprised of the elements of energy referred to as body, mind, and spirit, so too are there multiple levels to the vitality of Earth we refer to as Gaia. It is a strong trait in sentient life to be capable of seeing these connections of the physical and the spiritual realms.

The Mind of Gaia

Gaia's physical nature is readily discernible. It is the planet itself where you all exist while incarnate. The interplay and complex relationships of all living matter coupled with the geological and meteorological aspects of existence are becoming quite well studied, and breakthroughs of new understanding are on the horizon. Knowledge of growth cycles and seasons, tides, and air streams all grant a level of comprehension unique to humanity.

Most of the difficulties that the world is currently facing are often the result of a sense of superiority of humankind over nature. The idea that nature can be manipulated or altered begins with good intentions. A quest to make people safer or more secure may be the stated goal, but over-engineering the planet leads to massive flooding and increases earthquakes. It is far better to adapt to Gaia than to seek to control that which you do not understand. As we said earlier, there will soon be new ways to understand the interconnectedness of Earth's systems. It will prove to be a difficult thing to ignore.

Likewise, the life that is Gaia carries with it the energy of a mind. This is not exactly the same as the mind of a human, but it is similar in many ways. A human possesses a bicameral brain, and this is often mistakenly thought to be the complete entity referred to as the mind. However, this leaves out the most vital aspect of what separates humanity from most other life forms—that is, the heart, or the emotional aspect. Whereas the brain is the seat of logic and is powerful, the heart is where the sense of appropriate action toward other life forms begins. For far too long humanity has relied first and foremost on the logic side. This is a prime reason why there is the strong desire to think of, and often force, solutions rather than to simply feel or sense through intuition what is the appropriate path to follow. The heart, when allowed to lead and respond to inspiration, will most often make the correct choices in any decision that needs to be made. Together the heart and the brain—the emotional and the logical centers—can make the connection of the spiritual concerns to the physical matters, the "above" to the "below" as it were.

In the current day, much of the trouble on the planet can be seen as a subversion of the heart, or core emotional center of humanity. This can be most clearly seen in the way women have been subjected and treated as inferior over the centuries. Much of the social progress being made today can be directly traced back to strong women and men who allow themselves to be guided by strong women. Yin energy then leads yang energy and the result is growth and cooperation.

What, then, is Gaia's mind? How do we know what Gaia senses by way of logic or emotion? Can it be true that planet Earth has emotions, feelings, or opinions about things? We tell you now that the answer is strong in the affirmative. Yes, Gaia possesses a sense of what is best for all her life forms. She looks at all activity that takes place upon and within her sphere through a variety of means. Some of these means are through human eyes, but she does not rely solely on such limited vision. Some of her observations come through the eyes of her creatures, large and small. Even here, there is a limit as to what can be learned.

How Gaia Communicates

Much of Gaia's communication operates at a very deep level, unnoticed by her higher life forms. She is full with water, and it is here that she receives the maximum of her vibrations of communication. Much of these vibrations are not solely from her life on the planet but rather signals from the vast solar system and beyond into the galaxy. You see, the interconnectedness of life is far more than merely what exists on Earth itself. In a sense, Gaia speaks to and hears from her sibling planets and the star that guides and provides them with life-giving energies.

Gaia communicates with her own life forms. It is a wide variety, complex and diverse, that populates this good Earth. The primary key to comprehending how Gaia communicates is through that word itself, "communicate." The root of the term is "commune," and the sister word then becomes "community." Here we see one of the primary paths to communication. Wherever you see a natural community, you can be assured there is Gaian communication going on.

Consider ants or bees. Their very existence is based on an industrious and complex community. It could be said that their communities are perpetually communicating. But it extends beyond that. The bees themselves act as a type of messenger for Gaia, carrying information from trees and plants all about the world. Through those messages, there is continued growth. That growth carries the energy of interconnectedness, and through the bees' existence, all Gaia's life forms are influenced for the benefit of all. Imagine that the bees are a type of neural impulse that carries a single bit of information. Then take the next step and recall that there are millions of bees in flight at all times, all across the globe. This is one aspect of Gaia's mind and thought process.

What would happen to humans if their neural network began to be devoid of information? What if your senses were blocked or your brain suddenly limited in how much information was available? Currently there is great concern regarding the loss of the bee population. The interruption of Gaia's thought patterns will have an effect on all life. Currently there is a growing attempt by some of humanity to provide new stations and homes for bees to create their central hives. These are sensitive areas that pick up and receive the vibrations Gaia chooses to send. The same is true with ant colonies, only they sense things at a deeper level that is more profound. In a very real way, we can compare the ground-dwelling creatures to the brain while the creatures of the air correspond more rightly to the emotional state of Gaia.

How You Can Communicate Gaia's Will

Any small being that creates a high vibration while communicating or even just going about their daily tasks is truly a part of Gaia's mind. For a member of the family human, this knowledge can benefit you in energetic and subtle ways. Pausing in your day to meditate while in the woods or a forest can offer you the opportunity to hear what Gaia thinks and feels. Imagine that you are still and communing with natural things when a hummingbird or a dragonfly approaches your physical location. By allowing the creature to come near, by relaxing your energies, you could sense the mission this single tiny life form carries through the air. Be cautious not to focus too hard, for the little beings (the bees and also the small birds, as well as many insects too tiny to readily notice) are sensitive to your vibrations as well. If your emotions become too intense, they will quickly leave the area. If, however, you are practiced at quieting your heart and brain, they might come before you and pass along Gaia's wisdom. Of course, they carry only small bits of information. Yet constant practice and attendance on your part will increase these moments, bringing you closer into harmony with Earth's systems.

This can be true in other ways as well. Tending to plants or meditation with crystals and minerals can bring Gaian thought or emotion to you. This will be slower in some ways, but it could be easier for many members of the family human. A plant or crystal will not depart the area no matter how agitated or excited you become! Still, the path to communication with Gaia is always one of stillness and listening. Remember that listening is not done simply with your ears. A deeper vibration brings information to your consciousness. Consistency is key to gaining this skill.

There also is a higher vibrational communication, the aspect called spirit. Does Gaia have a spiritual nature? You can find the answer by pondering this: Do you believe that you have a spiritual nature? You belong to Gaia; that is, you are made of her elements. These elements come together in a wide diversity of life forms, yet no life form is composed of anything that is not found within Gaia. The human is often considered unique amongst Gaia's life forms, and this is a true statement. The reason is not that there are no other creatures that feel love or a sense of time or the ache of loss at the passing of a loved one. Many beings feel these emotions deeply. You do not consistently recognize them the way you do in each other, but they are there.

These beings who feel love are also sensitive to spiritual matters. They do not dwell so deeply as the family human does on matters considered metaphysical, but they do feel the realm of spirit in their own way. And they too are part of the cycle of karma—that is, death and rebirth and the filtering of energies through the systems of Earth.

If Gaia's life possesses a spiritual nature, Gaia herself— the source of your physical being—must then also be capable of a spiritual vibration. It occurs in this way: As the system of planets spirals through the galactic cluster, there is continual communication that arrives from the community of stars and planets as well as other physical matter that also makes up the Universe. Gaia, and indeed the entire solar system, speaks of the experiences, the thoughts and feelings, they carry. These thoughts and feelings are brought to consciousness from the smallest of elements and creatures to the more complex beings and communities that reside on not only Earth but also the complete community that you are truly a small part of.

Yet small does not mean unimportant. There is a preciousness to human life just as there is to other higher vibrationally situated animals. There is a special nature to those who not only sense spiritual things but also communicate them with one another. Here you may ask yourself: "What is it that I communicate? What words, thoughts, and emotions do I emanate from my karmic core? What vibrational level do I exist at, and what do I radiate from my true self? Is Gaia actively using me to commune with her life forms?"

Not all of humanity carries out Gaia's communication. Not all of humanity seeks to commune with Gaia. In this way, not all of humanity is contributing to Gaia's purpose of growth and diversity. Understand, she has her opinions and feelings about certain actions being taken by her life forms. She senses through her communities who and what are practicing peaceful processes and promoting paths of growth for all life.

Gaia senses where beings feel joy at being alive and express such joy by cooperating with her ecosystems, strengthening and supporting her rather than seeking to bend her to their will. She understands and feels the sense of love that many offer as they embrace the bounty and beauty Gaia provides willingly. Gaia senses, above all, the greater community of the Universe. She feels strongly the Source energy that courses throughout all creation. And Gaia brings that sense of Source to her life forms, all of us, both on Earth and to those who are in the realm of spirit near the planet.

It is left up to each of us to pause, be still, and listen with our hearts, and then we can take the appropriate actions Gaia requests for all our benefit. Fill your lives with the elements of love, joy, and especially peace, and then pause to hear what Gaia says to you. In this way, others will be able to hear what Gaia says through you.

6
Purifying Your Communication

As ABOVE, SO BELOW. When we speak these words, we are indicating something by its specific vibration. There are many languages in the Universe, and not all of them are conveyed with mere sound. In fact, there is more communication occurring in the Universe via vibrations other than sound. Yet while you are incarnate on the planet, your primary communication form is through speaking and hearing.

In a sense, all vibration is a communication. Since all things possess a vibrational quality, we can say that the Universe is in a constant state of communication or communing. When Source began this Universe, it started from a pure form of energy and swiftly transferred itself into a vast diversity of vibrational alterations and changes.

When the poet said, "In the beginning was the word," the poet understood that the first and continuing action of Source is to commune with itself. As all things (including you) are aspects and particles of Source, then all things, especially the sentient aspects of Source such as yourself, are in a continuum of communication.

With this in mind, when we say, "As above, so below," you can begin to clearly comprehend the scope of this statement. Despite the variety and diversity of the Universe, all things (matter and space) began and will end with a pure harmonious energy.

As you observe the fractious nature of human society today, you might rightly question whether harmony is even possible on Earth. We have spoken before of the phases of energy that Earth has passed through in the past several decades. The terms often applied to these times by many spiritually minded beings are Harmonic Convergence, Harmonic Concordance, and now the Harmonic Coalescence. Each is a small motion toward a time when many will be in sympathetic accord with one another. We are a long way off from all beings acting in total agreement, but the discord you are experiencing is nearing the conclusion of a cycle. Once finished, such disharmonious energy will not be witnessed again for a great amount of time.

A Time of Self-Examination

It is important for all beings on the planet to ask themselves, "Am I acting in such a way that I create a vibration that others can align to? Am I willing to listen and learn the peaceful vibrations of others? Am I capable of hearing the new song of Gaia, Earth itself?"

In this present day and age, there is a great movement sweeping across Earth. Humanity is caught in a whirling spiral of energy that began simply as a need for self-expression. What started as a path to equality for many humans who were unjustly pressed down in unbalanced societies now is a chaotic storm caused by old, unbalanced yang energy seeking to preserve its dominance over all things.

Above you—that is, in the realm of the spirit—we have felt the overactive yang seek to control yin. In reality, yin does not need to be controlled, and yang exists in a much more effective state when appropriately matched with yin. That this is occurring throughout this section of the galaxy may not be fully comprehended by those who are on Earth. This imbalanced energy has been the primary focus of many of the beings who exist "as above" in the spiritual realm. This has been our focus for quite a long time.

We act "above," and you then act "below" primarily by raising your own vibrations and setting a purifying intention for your lives. Only on Earth have you recently been able to begin to balance this energy. When we say "recently," we mean the past five hundred years. From a human standpoint, that is a great length of time. Yet this illustrates how great and long lasting this imbalance has been. Collectively, we will not wait nearly as long to see clear results and a strong path to equality for all humanity or observe many other beings on Earth grow and flourish.

Appropriate Words

First, though, those who are already of a mind to seek and exist in a state of higher vibrational living need to purify their own energies in the art of communication. It is a difficult thing in these times to remain neutral and peaceful in the face of such a great quantity of self-serving rhetoric and bitter rivalry. Yet this is what will set you apart and propel you forward into the future.

We have said before, "Do not waste your words." By offering this advice, we do not mean to remain silent in the face of oppression or injustice. What we do mean is that there is worthy communication and then there is also mere chatter. Much of the words being used today come into being by reaction. They are not thought out at all. The structure of so many ersatz communications is often weak and spasmodic, merely saying something for the sake of saying something. The value of such words is diminished, and by extension, so is the value of the speaker.

The culmination of much of the balancing work we have been engaged in offers a greater opportunity for self-expression. A byproduct from these efforts is that many humans feel a great need to be important beyond their actual roles in the karmic tapestry. It is not necessary to have an opinion on everything. In fact, you can gain strength by pulling your personal energies back inward and becoming still and quiet.

This state of stillness is not necessarily silence, nor is it an unmoving state. Rather, it is a path to discovery regarding your true nature. By pausing before you speak or react to outside stimuli, you will find that you will not need to add anything to a discussion. You will find that such conversations actually weigh you down and muffle your personal vibrational growth. It is not always necessary to engage in conversation with people who say derogatory or inflammatory things. Often your silence will allow them to access their own thoughts at a deeper level. This offers them the opportunity to raise their own vibration as well.

This course can be difficult. Where is the line between allowing unjust behavior to continue and taking a stand for spiritual principles? It is a hard thing to define. Some interesting aspects to ponder are: Do spiritual principles need defending? Will the truth eventually win out without your mental and verbal involvement? Or will the encounter become an entanglement for your heart and brain, drawing your mind away from true spiritual process?

We remind you now that cosmic balance is attained one being at a time. And the only person you can truly balance is yourself. In seeking higher vibrational living, you will find yourself in rarified society. The higher the levels you attain on your spiritual path, the fewer the people you will encounter on the planet who can truly communicate with you.

Yet there is greater communication available to ones who seek such a life. By freeing yourself from lower vibrational chatter, you will gain the opportunity to hear the sounds of the Universe. By purifying your own abilities to listen by removing the distractions of meaningless words and philosophies, the sense of connection to Source energies will clarify. It is not for the weak to engage in such forms of communing.

Spiritual Community

Today far too many members of the family human seek to be "right" in their opinions. In so doing, they do not uplift other beings. Rather, they press down others who possess the same needs and legitimacy of existence that they do. This is the old energy that is being brought into balance "above" in the spiritual realm and in great swaths of the galaxy. Earth is now prepared for such a balancing. Are you?

You are a vital aspect of this activity! By seeking to gain balance yourself, you place yourself in line with these cosmic powers. The purer your communication—that is, the purer your vibration—the more harmony you will feel and display. The opportunities to speak will arise, as others who also seek balance will be drawn to you and you to them. The numbers will swell, and as the balancing proceeds, the spiritual population of Earth will not be so spread apart.

Generationally, a strong shift is occurring right now. Much of the wasted opportunities for communication are no longer being tolerated by energetic youth. They desire to create a new place of growth and harmony for themselves and their children. For the first time in many years, the energy has shifted to allow for rapid alterations to all human society.

Humanity appears to be mired in hatred and in sectarian attitudes. Yet the generations now taking their place as leaders of society are following a higher calling based on principles of fulfillment and happiness rather than dominance and exploitation. Many of you have witnessed great strides forward for the family human. These have been, at their core, propelled by the cause of love, and there is no greater power. The result is often a glimpse of a future of joy and peace. Fix this vision in your minds.

Open your core being to commune with the Universal Source. Leave behind petty bickering regarding who or what is the absolute right path for humanity and Earth. That path is being decided on at a higher level. Ponder and emanate the spiritual qualities of love, joy, and peace. In this way, you balance and purify yourself and give space for others to join you in spiritual communication.

7
Messengers to the Future

AS ABOVE, SO BELOW. In these opening words, we set an expectation. The realm of spirituality possesses a similar type of existence to that experienced in the physical realm. This is often a truth in principle more than in a practical reality. The principles, however, can be illustrative and grant the spiritual seeker a higher perspective, leading them to a strong potential to personally exist within a higher vibration, even while living in the lower vibrational physical realm.

Spiritual beings that exist outside of the realm of gravity and physical weight are often thought of in a variety of ways. For much of recorded history humanity has thought us to be guides or angels. The implication of such titles is that we carry a message to those who are capable of hearing it. Though there is much more involved in our role, there is truth to this thought. Are you such a one who is capable of hearing us?

Choosing to Receive

As you receive words and thoughts from angels and guides, you are affected by the source of the message offered. You are not bound to the message. It is information, and you have the opportunity to act on it or allow it to remain unactivated in your life.

A true spiritual message will carry no sense of judgment for the recipient. In the higher realms, we understand that all actions taken result in consequences. When a being chooses not to act on information presented, that choice then prompts the consequence. The choosing or not choosing is the action.

Actions taken in the past have brought about the societies you live in today. At any given moment, things could have gone quite differently, and the world could possibly be on a path that you cannot fully comprehend from where you currently exist. In the past, many spiritual messages were delivered, and many were twisted far from their original intent.

What is true, however, is that despite the choices made by myriad humans throughout hundreds of centuries, there has been a strong current of energy carrying humanity along in a very specific direction. Those who hear and act on the messages delivered from the realm of spiritual beings will find that their own vibrational beings are raised to a higher level.

By raising your own personal vibration, you purify the path for others, releasing the density that many sense in the physical world today. The sooner this lower vibrational energy is loosened and allowed to flow, the sooner the feeling of blockage will be released and the feeling of freedom can fully develop in human society.

Taking Personal Responsibility
for the Messages You Receive

Allowing others to interpret and dictate messages for you, an individual being with full ability to make a spiritual choice, could cause a delay in the goal of a peaceful and progressive future for all beings on the planet. In the past, societies might have received strong spiritual guidance, but the message was often subverted for the sake of gaining power over others. In the current day and the years to come, this will be less likely as humanity and Gaia both raise their vibrations in a concurrent manner.

The passage to peace and a true new age is gaining momentum. Many humans, as well as other sentient beings on and around Earth, are gaining strength and conviction as they travel that path to a future of increased spiritual living. In the past, many heard the messages, but few adhered to the true sentiment stated. Today, many hear the messages and, by their actions, become messengers themselves.

Where Do Messages Come From?

Worthy messengers do not create the messages they deliver. They also do not decide whether the messages are worthy. The responsibility they possess is one that is earned, for they are faithful in their duty. They might not even fully comprehend the message. They exist as messengers to take the thoughts and emotions of one being to another or perhaps from a group to many others.

Once delivered, the message is a potential energy. If not acted on, the message's power will dissipate. By repeating the message, it can retain its potential, but it is only through heeding the information or guidance given that the message becomes alive.

It is said that one should not kill the messenger. In this maxim, we see that the recipients might not like or agree with the message delivered, and it is, again, not the messenger's fault. The messenger only acts as an envoy from one party to another. It is the responsibility of the recipients to accept or reject what they hear. There is no system of punishment or reward for an individual's actions. There is only consequence.

Words that raise the vibration of humanity today stem from the realm we refer to as "above." It is a common misunderstanding that there is one higher being in charge of everything. All sentient beings are aspects of a higher consciousness, and as such, we are all creating the present and the future moments. Yet there are those in the realm above—the spiritual realm—that have a far greater vision and perception. By listening to them (hearing and heeding the foresight they have gained from long eras spent gaining wisdom through knowledge and experience), we can benefit. And by repeating and amplifying the messages, we too are speakers of higher vibrational guidance. This, then, is the easiest path to gaining the higher spiritual nature that is within the grasp of all humanity in the coming decades.

Twisting the message for your own purpose carries the opposite consequence. We say this again: There are far fewer beings alive on the planet today that will follow such twisted messages than there were in the past. The filtering that occurs in the realm of gravity is active and working.

As a channel, or bearer of a spiritual message, the being speaking or writing the words of that message is often allowed to craft the thoughts to increase clarity or the potential for better understanding. This carries a greater responsibility, and the channel oftentimes is considered an ambassador of the spiritual realm. There is a greater weight of responsibility to this position of ambassador than to that of messenger.

In the current day and age, we are entering a point where the future is becoming clearer. The choices that all sentient beings on Earth will be making in the coming decade have an increased sense of importance. It is important to hear the messages correctly.

Types of Messages

Two specific kinds of message are going to be increasing in the near future. First, there is predictive vision. This is tricky, and we caution everyone now to receive this type of communication carefully. It is tempting to interpret the signs that are seen. Often your personal fears will come into play. Gloom and doom may be the result of such information, and we can clearly see from past experience that this was a common reaction. Fear-based predictions often do not have any true basis in reality. There have been warnings of the end of the world or supernatural vengeance descending on one culture's or religion's enemies. Yet the world does not end. The world and humanity continue and thrive. There are dark times when disasters might occur. These are not caused by supernatural beings. Belief in this way is not a sign of a mature spiritual person but rather a low-vibrational, fear-based culture.

When examining a vision of the future, it is good to follow certain guidelines. Keep in mind that any spiritual message will carry with it information allowing for growth. There will be thoughts of coming peace within the vision. There will be reality, of course, but when a difficult change is witnessed, the true spiritual message will not cease at that point. Pay attention to see beyond the difficulties. The beings sending the message are doing so with the hope that the hearers will take heart and assist others to carry on in the face of what might be great changes.

The second form of message will be one of guidance. These will be more common. In fact, there is an abundance of such communication available to the discerning spiritual seeker already. The true spiritual communicator will offer awareness and preparation guidance—aware and prepare.

True communicators will not use fear. They will know and follow the principle that beings must accept or reject the information offered on their own.

True spiritual communicators will recall that it is not their responsibility to lead and expect others to follow. They will see clearly that their task is simply to communicate. Their communication will be marked by the qualities of love and joy. They will clearly bring peaceful feelings to the listener. In the future, all humans will carry the weight of being responsible for their own course. That time is fast approaching.

The balance of Earth's future depends on this single thing: the release of the need to be in control of others and Earth itself. An understanding that humanity is a small aspect of the natural course of the Universe will go far in bringing peace to the karmic family that each one of us is a part of.

Though we possess sentience, that does not make us in charge. It only offers the energy of Source a conscious vision of itself.

Observe and exist, witness and experience, and participate and enjoy; this is the ultimate communication skill that angels and guides will use to bring the large message to humankind. Living in a way that expresses love to others, holds joy in existence, and radiates peace to all on Earth is the highest form of spiritual growth available to those incarnate on Gaia.

8

Cosmic Consciousness
and a Sense of Scale

AS ABOVE, SO BELOW. With these words, we acknowledge the perceived separation that many in the family human possess. Yet, you comprehend the ability to communicate with one another from points at a great distance from each other on the planet. In some cases, it is simple and an accepted reality through the use of technology. Why, then, doubt the ability to communicate using only what energies you inherently possess?

Can you truly contact beings who are not physical? To do so, a being must first allow a broader perception of the Universe.

Communication with Beings
beyond the Physical Realm

As spiritual beings, we are drawn to the peculiarity of this communication, this channeling of our thoughts into words. Humans who accomplish this type of communication must overcome the notion that we are at some distant place. In the physical realm, you exist without the ability to fully comprehend the Universe as it truly is, as a dimensional entity beyond the three and the four dimensions that are often imagined. Because of this, it can seem that there is some distant place for beings in the spirit realm to dwell, yet the spirit realm is a place that you also exist, that we exist, where everything exists. It is only in the lower vibrational realms that you are unable to perceive what is happening in a realm of higher vibration: a realm of light, certainly, but more than light—beyond light.

This Realm of Light beyond light is where energy exists at its primary nature, and it is manipulated easily and often. Yet at the lower vibration, where you exist, it seems as if energy is not manipulated as easily. The perception you might have, then, is not that energy cannot be manipulated but rather that it is a time-based action for you beings that inhabit a physical body, a lower vibrational body in a lower vibrational world within a solar system that consists of mass and gravities. That is where you currently exist. In that lower vibrational realm, most life does not try to manipulate energy. But you do.

The reason you do, as a human being, is that you are also quite directly connected to the consciousness of the Source. You have a vision of the future. You have a remembrance of the past. Most life in gravitational realms do not carry or assign importance to these things.

So, why do we choose this topic now? There are many unexpected shifts and alterations on the planet these days. The uncertainty factor of life and existence is one that cannot be fathomed at your level.

As we in the spirit realm manipulate energy from the higher realms, the consequences to the lower realms can be dramatic and in some cases traumatic. This is true even to those who are seeking a higher level of perception, a higher level of vibration, even to those who prepared for such changes in a philosophical, spiritual way. And as manipulated energies create ripple effects, as these things draw down to the gravitational well you exist in, what we in the spiritual realm envision as progress, as process, as projects headed toward completion, you in the physical realm envision as something coming out of the clear blue sky, as it were.

There are greater patterns at work. So as climates change, as human emotions change, as the Sun spirals through the galaxy, Earth and thus humanity enter into different phases of energy, different areas, and different spaces. You are simply unable to see the larger pattern unless you are in a higher vibrational state. Comprehension of the Universe is not possible from the perception that you have. What you can comprehend is the mis-comprehension of the Universe that you have with your own perception.

In this is the beginning of a wider, broader understanding, a sense of smallness on your part, an awesome sense of scale, yet in awe there is truth. In the state of awe, there is the realization of how interconnected things actually are. Your vibration rises when you reach those moments where you feel the holistic quality of nature—of things that are natural, of things in the physical realm, of which the Universe is a thing in the physical realm.

The Universe, being the physical realm that it is, actually exists within the spiritual realm. Oh! How big must the spiritual realm be for your Universe to fit within? And if you think your Universe is infinite and still fits within the spiritual realm, then is the spiritual realm somehow more than infinite? Are there multiple Universes within the spiritual realm? The easy answer to that is yes. The more difficult answer to that is in describing how Universes exist. Within this Universe that you exist in, it is a matter of perception and vibration, and it is a matter of what often is called magic.

The multidimensional aspects of everything are imponderables to even the greatest minds, yet they do ponder. They look for the mathematics of it all, and in the mathematics, there will be proof. In so many ways, the multidimensional aspects have already been proven, and the greatest minds do not even know it because they cannot see it because perception is reality and then reality becomes perception. So whatever the accepted reality is becomes the standard and accepted perception. It is very difficult to break through that.

Beyond the Veil of Perception

As spiritual beings, we are not entirely comfortable with the term "the veil" because it is not an accurate term. We will, however, use the term "veil" for it does approximate the concept.

This Veil of Perception is a thin membrane. It is gauzy, and it can be seen through. The closer you get to it, the brighter the light appears on the other side. It can be pierced. It can be raised. It can be lowered. Yet we are speaking in a purely three-dimensional and four-dimensional way by assigning it a physical nature. It is no such thing, but we will stick with the term.

A being can move up to the limitation that the veil represents. A being can press against it, and in a certain way, a being can interact with the dimensions that the other side of the veil represents—especially if there is a consciousness on the other side of the veil that understands that someone is trying to interact, that a sentient being is seeking interaction.

As Onereon, we are not predictive. In this era, in this place that the planets are in, we hesitate to hazard guesses about what might happen on the planet. We see the larger patterns. We see the efforts, in some cases taken on our behalf but truly taken on behalf of others in the spiritual realm, larger entities than we. We see them, and we play our role.

Most often our role is completely invisible. Most often the guidance that we give is taken without notice. Prayers are answered, comfort is offered, blessings are delivered, aspects of life shift with manifestation, wider perception is granted, and other techniques get the credit. It is part of our mandate to not be noticed in so many instances. If beings start to realize the consciousness behind the answering of their prayerful requests or who is delivering manifestation energies, they start to think in terms of ownership. A tendency develops of a lack of responsibility on their behalf, and they do not act for themselves; they passively request action from others.

We say it is a beautiful world, but it is not a safe one. Particularly now, it is not a safe world. The uncertainty is what makes it unsafe.

Perspective and positive thinking, these are your strengths. Optimism for the future is a strength, and it is an appropriate use of energy. Optimism about the people around you is a strength, even when it does not occur and even when it is unfulfilled.

What Is the Point of It All?

It is an easy answer. The point is that Source set out to experience diversity, and the way that Source chose to experience diversity is to diversify itself. Thus, everything is Source. However, in that diversification, Source did not set limitations on what these experiences would be, so there are many experiences that interrupt other experiences, creating a sense of imbalance.

If you were to look at physical things spinning around the Sun, you will see that some of them do not orbit in a regular fashion. They come and they intercept and they interrupt other orbits. In very rare cases, the interruption is actually a physical collision, objects that are in space colliding with other objects.

On the whole, if you are not looking closely, you see how the solar system travels through the galaxy and the galaxy travels in a spiral of the Universe. It is all quite beautiful and quite balanced. On the whole, things are balanced. It is only when you get smaller and smaller and smaller that you see the effort it takes to maintain the larger balance of something like a galaxy or Universe.

In this section of the galaxy, there was a disturbance, an imbalance, and that energetic interaction is difficult to explain. That energy continues to exist and seeks balance. It is an aspect of Source. Source seeks balance. But Source also sought diversity and achieved it quite well. Now it struggles to regain balance and retain diversity.

Even we, Onereon, are too small. We do not clearly see how and when all of it will play out. Although it is a source of communication between us in the spiritual realm, we are also content to play our part. And to be truthful, we understand that all of the information we have just given is an interpretation and a perception, and there could yet be a much higher pattern that we can one day discern and a much greater reason for all of these things.

Searching for reason can be settled in this section of space-time in this way: Seek balance. Seek balance through motion. Image spiraling. We have said these words so many times. Seek the image of the spiral always. Rather than reason why, just look at what is.

In all things, understand that these communications between the spiritual and the physical realms are increasing. The interruptive energies seem to be taking us further away from balance. Still, the reality not yet beheld is one of peace. Understanding and believing this is called faith. Listen for your own guides or angels (or whatever term you choose to use). They are nearer than before. We are nearer than before.

Joy is the result of optimism for the future. It is a difficult thing for many to achieve these days.

Comprehend the reality and continue to strive for a joyful state. This is an appropriate use of energy.

In all, recall that the highest level of energy available to all beings is love. This is the light beyond light. You carry this infinite energy within you, and it is only your perception that limits this in your life. Look at the infinite. Allow awe to enter your daily existence. Love will follow, for there is nothing else.

9
Purifying Your Personal Path to Enlightenment

As ABOVE, SO BELOW. We always begin with these words. The words themselves are information. The information of "as above, so below" coincides with the concept of reincarnation, a returning to a planet.

When using the term "reincarnation," what we mean is the process of becoming part of the physical world, fulfilling your time, and then moving beyond the physical world. Your energy returns to a level, a realm, slightly higher than the gravity well that you are engaged in while you are on the planet. This is not a completely unique system; it happens other places in the galaxy and in the Universe as well. It is intensified around the planet Earth because we are working with an energy system, trying to purify and clarify some energy.

Purification of the Planet

In your physical lives, you are an aspect of karmic energy that is moving through a filter and, little by little, impurities, things that are imbalanced, are removed from you. Yet the world is not balanced. Society is not balanced.

So you also pick things up. The quest for balance is perpetual. It is what you do with those unbalanced thoughts, imbalanced feelings, and imbalanced situations that help to purify the energy.

Now, imbalanced situations that you encounter might be very small. It might be a single issue with another human being, or it could be something quick in passing. For example, when someone gets in your way physically in a social environment or an errand you might be running. It only takes seconds for them to be in and then out of your way. How do you deal with that? It is the balancing that you do at that moment, the releasing, the letting go, the allowing for someone else's flow.

Spiritually minded beings allow for flow of energy. You can start to see how small things can become large things because some people cannot let those things go. They feel those things. They bind themselves to those things. They carry those things and say, "That person got in *my* way!" By behaving in this manner, they stop their own flow, repeatedly, based on an event that is minor or relatively insignificant. Who knows what that other person was doing or where they were going.

To label or judge a situation or person as right or wrong can affect that person in small energetic ways, karmically speaking, but the greater effect is on you when you judge. When you say, "*That* person was incorrect. *That* person was wrong. *That* person was rude," maybe that person was none of those things. Maybe that person was just preoccupied with something important in his or her life.

Releasing your judgment is a balancing for you because judging—saying one thing is right or one thing is wrong—stops your flow of energy and stops the clear flow of energy that comes from Source. We remind you now that you are all particles of Source. You are all aspects of the creative energy of the Universe. Everything that makes up your life: your physical form, your thoughts, your emotions, your heart—everything, everything that makes those things up—comes from somewhere. It comes from the heart of the Universe.

When you feel tension at small, insignificant things, what are you creating? What do you bring into existence through tension, through small angers? You might not know that you are angry. You might not even understand what actually happened. Sometimes these things are insignificant. Awareness of who you are—how you think, your judgment, your path—is an important thing. Turning to yourself, examining yourself, thinking about yourself, and focusing on yourself will help you to see where there are stuck things, energy clogs.

Imagine a fine net being dragged through very, very dirty water. When you pull it out, what you see are a lot of clogs in the net. So you remove those things, and you put the net back in and drag it through the water again. We are purifying energy imbalances that occurred some thousands of years ago in this vicinity, on this planet, similar to the way you purify your water. It takes effort and time to clean the polluted water. The same is true for the unbalanced energies affecting Earth at this time.

Clean your net so that you can become more effective in the purification process, so that the area around you becomes more clear, more balanced. We see how we are mixing the terms "balance" and "purification." It is almost as if they are two separate things, but in fact they are two illustrations that cover one concept.

Gaining a Clear Path to Enlightenment

As a human being on the planet, you have an opportunity to make judgments. As a human being on the planet, you also have an opportunity to release judgment. Spiritual seekers often use the term "enlightenment." They wish to become enlightened. They pray for it. They meditate about it. They study. They seek the "path" to enlightenment. Ask yourself, "What keeps light from entering something?" Doors, walls, boundaries, physical things. Physical things will create shade, shadow, and darkness. So any time we structure an event with a label—a judgment—what are we doing? Preventing light from entering that area.

Ironically, what are we really good at while on the planet? Creating structures and disciplines! Defining ourselves by what we do and build. And we often find a way to label those as spiritual pursuits. Sometimes we label them by religious names: Christianity, Buddhism, Catholicism, the Islamic path. Sometimes we label things by the actions we take: movement disciplines such as tai chi or yoga. Sometimes we label ourselves by what we eat or do not eat. Sometimes we label ourselves by what we read. Sometimes we label ourselves by what we refuse to do. Here on the planet, sometimes people think that those labels help them to find enlightenment. Some even believe that the labels grant them spiritual status over others.

Ask yourself, "Where does the light come from?" The answer to that question is where you will find enlightenment. The answer is easy. Putting the knowledge to work is challenging. We have said this many times before. You are an element of the creative energy of the Universe. You are an aspect of Source. Thus, you are a carrier of creative light. Although you are on the planet, although you are in gravity, you have access to that creative energy. Act in a creative way, and that energetic light will begin to shine brighter around you.

When you say, "I am," you begin the creative process. When you release labels, you open the area around you to light. Again, where does light come from? Within the human being, there is light, and it radiates out. We are not talking specifically about physical light. We are talking about spiritual light. We are talking about that feeling of clarity, that feeling of brightness, that feeling of openness, and the sense of connection to Source. Can you imagine how that feels? Say the words, "I am creative. I am connected to Source. I am enlightened." Even if you do not feel this way, you have just begun the process to gain clearer access to this state of being.

So, are we saying that labels are wrong? You see how that judgment could happen? We are not saying that they are right or wrong. What we are saying is to notice where you label and notice where you create boundaries.

Now, none of those things that we mentioned is wrong. Also, none of them is right. Take away judgment of all of those things. If you choose a specific diet, that is fine. That is your path, then. You might look at other people, noticing their paths, and ask, "How do you do *this*, or how do you do *that*?" and they will give you information. They will give you ideas that could set you along a refreshed path. But if you say, "I want to do exactly what *this* person does." Well, you are not that person. Why would you do that? If you choose to move or act in a certain way, if you maneuver your physical form in a certain discipline—running or walking or standing or sitting or a making a posture—is that assisting you? Is that allowing you a greater flow? If the answer is yes, then do that. If that discipline is not easily assimilated into your life, then perhaps it is not in harmony with who you are at the moment. Do not feel obliged to follow any specific path.

Integrating disciplines into your own life is the act of taking a label and purifying. It is removing the judgments that become inherent in religious and spiritual practices and pursuits. It is removing the judgments that become inherent in dietary restrictions. It is removing the judgments. How is it doing that? Because you are doing it for yourself. It is an action that emanates from your core karmic level. It is who you are. There is no expectation for others to follow you or for you to follow others. In this way, you are radiating out your own light, and you do not expect other people to follow the labels that you create or promote.

Your path, then, is not a path. Think in terms of paths that you know. Perhaps you have visited a forest or a woodland, and there is an existing path, a place where many people or animals have walked and worn it down, generation after generation. You can follow that path. But what if you go somewhere and there is no path? There are, in every single day, places that no one has walked before.

You have that opportunity to step away and walk where no one has walked before. You create the path. The events that happen along the path might seem familiar to other people; they might have done similar things. You, this unique being—this being of the creative source of energy, of light—are coming along and perhaps doing familiar things, perhaps something that has been done for thousands of years. But because it is you and your perception of the world is different, it is a path that no one has taken. If you are conscious, if you are aware, if you look to see where you can push away labels, where you can purify, and where you can allow light into the situations then something as simple as going to a grocery store to acquire food can become a brand-new path. Everything you do can take on the element of enlightenment and spiritual growth.

A Continuing Path of Spiritual Existence

We are talking about a greater vision here. We are not talking about mundane things. Although those are the details, the single steps, that make up the journey. We are talking about your life, coming to the end of your life and saying, "I walked my path. I went where I wanted to go, not where other people tried to channel me. I did things my own way." When you come to the end of your life on the planet, it is not the end of your path. It is merely the end of the time you are to spend on the planet at this moment. When you come to that end, can you say you purified yourself and your surroundings as much as you possibly could? Did you create a balanced existence as much as you possibly could in an imbalanced world? When you have that last moment—the last breath that you take, the last liquid that you swallow, the last thing you see, the last smile you give—and you enter into the transformation from physical into spiritual once again, how much easier it will be if you are already in a balanced mode, not clinging to anything when you pass from this life on the planet.

We have work for you, when you pass from this life. You have responsibilities here in the spiritual realm. There are responsibilities at all vibrations and at every level. You are a conscious being. Your consciousness will remain a conscious being as you pass from gravity. It is not a vacation outside of the gravity well. But it is brighter. It is lighter.

Relinquish Judgment

How many labels do you create for other people? How many labels do you create for yourself? How many things do you do in a day that prevent enlightenment and inhibit your light from radiating out? Do not judge yourself. Let yourself be who you are. When you notice those things, laugh, because the best way to purify imbalance is not through anger but happiness. The spiritual energies that we all exist and grow under are never force, coercion, and guilt. No one grows from guilt. No one grows from fear. Eliminate those things from your life. Do not feel guilty. Feel grateful.

You are alive. Be grateful for this. Then build on that. Be grateful for that person who slows you down, because you do not know why that happened. Wish the person well. Help that person to be balanced by wishing him or her well. Do you see what you can do? You radiate out your light. Do not withhold it. It does not cost you a thing. The creative energy of the Universe—there is a lot of it. You cannot possibly use it up. The principles of that energy are always: diversity, appreciation, enjoyment, color, sound, concept, and creativity—always.

Thus, we encourage you to seek that higher level of spiritual existence. Eliminate, where you can, the labels. Integrate your practice to act without judgment. Raise your vibration by eliminating things that lower your vibration and that prevent you from vibrating at a higher rate—those heavy, heavy things such as guilt and fear and anger. If you are feeling guilty, change it to gratitude. It is as simple as that. If you feel fear, change it to love. It is as simple as that. It you are feeling anger, change that to acceptance or allowance. Let the energy flow. Follow your path. When something is in your way, go around it, and radiate your light of love as you do.

These actions create a being of balance. You will never be perfectly balanced while on the planet. There are just too many things happening. But the principles that we always speak about—joy, peace, and love—those are the driving forces that raise a being's vibration. Those are the driving forces that break everything else down. They are the primary energies of a spiritual being. They are the purest energies that you can have. They are the things that can emanate the easiest, and when you do it, they are the things that will return to you the swiftest and the fullest amounts available of Source energy, the creative energy of the Universe.

We remind you now of the words, the labels, but we encourage you to notice the spiritual energy of the concepts of love and joy and peace. Say them aloud. Say, "I am," and add these words: "love and joy and peace." Can you feel that?

10
Coping with a Lower Vibrational World

AS ABOVE, SO BELOW. Much diversity exists on planet Earth. The beauty and joy that can be experienced is exceptional in the known Universe. Why, then, are there many who do not feel good about life and living? Why is the sense of joy not present in a greater capacity in every human's life?

Many sense that there are individual moments when they should feel grateful or excited. Simple things that happen often (such as sunsets) or seasonal occurrences (such as the changing of leaves or the first snowfall or the first buds on the trees in spring) are often cited as points of life that should be appreciated fully. Likewise, reuniting with long-lost friends and family or welcoming new children into the world is joyful. Even the acquisition of a new pet or dwelling place is cause for joy.

But these things can become mundane in a crowded world, filled with images of the events being used to sell products or manipulate emotions in monetary transactions. The individual human in the current age has become jaded and cautious with his or her emotional responses. This is a defense that has great purpose, but any defense is also something that shields a being from others. The massive invasion of needless imagery or mindless entertainment is taking its toll on human society. It does not bring us together in the sense of being united in a common cause. Rather, it herds us together as if we are merchandise to be put upon a shelf.

The Weight of the World

There is a lowering of vibration that occurs. It happens when there are too many conflicting vibrations cancelling out the higher, more spiritual frequencies. For many, this is a choice. They choose to accept such a rush of imagery because it seems (and often is) easier than engaging their intellect and critically thinking about each element of information being presented.

The human brain is a sensitive thing. It receives so much by way of sensory content, more than simply sight, sound, smell, taste, and touch. In an effort to protect itself, the mental process will often accept the easiest path. The dominant information, that which is repeated most often, is accepted as true and important. The brain also looks at what is happening in the community. It will compare the surrounding world, noting what the rest of the tribe of humans nearby is accepting, and then follow the path of least resistance. This allows the individual to fit in and live amongst others, granting a feeling of acceptance and protection.

What follows is that the individual begins to conform to the lowest common denominator offered. For a spiritually minded person, this cannot continue for long, for a spiritual seeker is already attuned to higher vibrational communication. They naturally sense where the true elements of life exist. It is not within masses of people. It is not found during events of conflict, whether staged or real. It is not found in ancient religions of oppression and imbalance. Yet each of these arenas carries the lower vibrational, deadening action that will quell the higher vibrational spiritual nature of an individual human.

There is a reason that changing seasons and moments of great beauty (such as a sunrise or a full moon) grant a peaceful sensation to the human experience. There is a reason that meeting ones of like heart action, those we are connected to at a deep emotional and karmic level, gives us a strong emotional burst of love. There is a reason that the sight of a new child causes involuntary smiles and even tears and laughter. These are times when the realm of spirit is close.

The higher vibrational aspects of being more purely connected to Source energies grant great cleansing power to the weighty concerns that the imbalanced world artificially creates. The feelings of love, peace, and joy in these moments lift the heavier, lower vibrations and allow us access to a better path of life on Earth. Seeking such experiences is the natural way of a spiritual human. Supplanting them with artificial anger or reveling in manufactured conflicts is an abdication of the greatest gift a human possesses — that of creating oneself in the harmonious path of Source energy.

Those who cut themselves off from such higher vibrational experiences miss much. But it is not for one to judge another's decision in this regard. For many, there is simply not the strength within to maintain the struggle of accessing higher vibrational lifestyles. Casting judgment on such ones merely accentuates or adds to their burden. Expressing love to such ones offers them opportunity for comparison of their paths to the path of the one who exhibits love. This, then, is also a way for each to achieve access to higher vibrations.

Seeking to Resist the Lower Vibrations

There are those who are well aware of the need to increase spirituality in their lives. Yet they seem to consistently slip back into the heavier vibrations. We tell you now, never before has there been such a strong pull to return to old patterns and paths on Earth. We are—all of us in the realm of spirit as well as in the realm of gravity—sensing the final moments of power that set the human society on such an imbalanced course for so many thousands of years.

Ones who seek to attain happiness and creative lifestyles yet continually spiral downward into depression are stronger than they realize. The struggle they experience is very real. The energies they work with and against are subtle. The purification they are undergoing is intense, and not all of them succeed by earthly standards. But they often are succeeding by the spiritual perception. Indeed, they might be the ones most admired by their guides and spiritual companions.

The world is a series of conflicting vibrations. Many of these ones, those facing depression or worse, are strongly empathic. They sense far more than anyone realizes. Their ability to shut out such vast psychic noise is limited. They seek solitude quite often out of self-defense. Because of this, they are often viewed as weak or not valuable to the rest of human society. In a sense, they are the ones leading the way into the future.

Much of the seeds of the current challenges lie in the simple fact that there are far too many humans clustered in specific areas of Earth. Too many humans and not enough resources have created a world of tension and uncertainty. This vibrational chaos is affecting the global community in an adverse way. The simple day-to-day struggle for supplies invokes such strong uncertainty that when compressed and amplified by tens of thousands of humans in a small, densely populated area, the mindset shifts easily to fear, which in turn feeds anger.

Entering a Time of Balance

This is what is shifting now. The realization that there is an alternative way of life is being not just understood but also pursued by the current generations maturing in the present day. They are not looking to the older generations for assistance any longer. They are creating their own communities. With the use of technology, they begin to comprehend that they do not need to remain in dense population centers. The beings who inhabit the great cities are looking at alternatives—not just moving away from them, but also making them more livable.

These ones are making more conscious choices in their lives, especially regarding the aspect of procreation. Many put off the creation of families until they themselves felt prepared for this responsibility. They are greeting their children with a new acceptance, allowing these new earthlings to be who they are rather than force them to behave as a cohesive artificial unit.

Those who face depression are examples for many who wish to create and live within a more productive, equal, more spiritually connected global community. They themselves do not think in terms of spirituality, yet they practice the principles long associated with such a path.

They do not seek to judge others. Rather, they seek to understand one another. They do not seek to gain from others at the expense or lessening of another's life. Rather, they seek cooperative enterprises that inform and increase entire communities. They do not feel the call to possess or own vast empires. They seek and enjoy prosperity and look for ways to allow others to also share in an abundant world.

This way is different from what has been experienced on the planet for well over seven thousand years. Yet it is not a different way for all human existence. There once was a time of balance with the planet and with all life forms, and the ones who seek a higher vibration will hear karmic echoes of those days.

Despite the difficulties humanity faces each day of this challenging age, there are still moments of joy to be experienced. Take advantage of the daily, seasonal aspects of change and the cycles of growth and dormancy. Look to these aspects of Gaia as examples for your own lives.

Seek a more natural path when possible, but take pleasure in what is at hand for you in your present situations. Be creative and enjoy others' creativity. In this way, you are supporting the primary energy of Source.

Release the need to judge the world. In this way, you will recall peace into your heart. As you raise your vibrations, even if you seem to fail at times, and as you continue to seek a mode of growth, you will find that there is love available from the Universe itself—for Source is love.

You are an aspect of Source. Love comes from within you. Begin with yourself.

11
Balancing Yin and Yang

AS ABOVE, SO BELOW. Often we are asked why the world is so unbalanced. Why does it seem that certain humans can be of the highest spiritual nature when others of the human species appear to be exactly the opposite, more animalistic or self-serving? These questions, when asked, show marvelous awareness on the part of the questioner. This awareness is the beginning of a path of wisdom and enlightenment that many would do well to follow. It can be a convoluted path, true, but this should not deter the spiritual seeker. We in the spirit realm also find ourselves pondering the nature of the family human.

Vibrational Reality

In the realm of spiritual existence, we strive to operate from a balanced yin and yang energetic. The vital nature of the Universe is more easily balanced when out of the influence of gravity. Those personalities that you call guides and angels are beings of a higher vibrational existence, but they are still operating near Earth and the solar system. They too are affected by gravity, but not nearly to the extent that you are while incarnate in the physical realms.

Vibrational existence is more of a spectrum, or a varied field of energetic reality. Imagine a prism refracting white light into many colors, or a rainbow. There is a definite place that one might call blue or green, but before coming to that determination, there is a shade lighter or darker of the primary designation, and after close examination, there is no clear delineation from one color to the next. It is this way in existence and hence the reason we use the phrase "as above, so below." There might appear to be a sharp division between life on Earth and life off the planet, but that is more a manufactured perception of reality than truth.

In other words, we in spirit are closer to you incarnate on Earth than many are capable of believing. The number of beings alive in the realm of gravity with the ability to discern spiritual beings is increasing. There is still clarity and comprehension missing, but as generations continue, the illusion of separateness will fade, and the reality will become clear to those who are not trained out of their natural vision. The ability to communicate with beings in the physical and spiritual realms will return. The balance of yin and yang at this time will be vastly improved. Until then, we see a continued imbalance. Why is this?

In the past, there was a period of intense yang energy that the solar system and, in a lesser sense, this arm of the galaxy, passed through. The immediate effect was one of potential destruction. Rather than begin a long process of crafting life cycles again, Source energy, in the form of spirit beings, understood the wisdom of filtering and dissipating the overabundance of yang energy. From the perspective of a human lifespan, this overly yang influence seems to have gone on for far too long. Even from the perspective of those in the lower ranges of spiritual existence, it feels as if we have been at this process too long. Yet the higher one is in vibrational existence, the easier it is to withstand and fully comprehend the progressive and balancing path we are on.

When we say "we," the meaning is all sentient life on or around planet Earth and the solar system. You see, it is not just Gaia who is involved in the process. There are many others engaged in this filtering activity. They remain in the outer reaches of the solar system, however, distancing themselves from the gravity well of the Sun. This is important, for they hold energy for the future of humanity and the healing and nurturing of future generations. It is kept pure at a distance. Occasionally and with increasing regularity, there are pulses of this pure and fresh energy being sent toward the inner planets.

This is why there is an increase in spiritually aware beings on Earth. It is also why there is a seeming concentration of overly yang energies at this time. In truth, what is occurring is that the imbalanced yang is being contained and concentrated so that it too can be refreshed and gain a balanced purification.

An Appropriate Balance

Remember that yin and yang exist in everything. It is true that some things are stronger in one than another. This is an appropriate arrangement. When balanced, neither seeks to dominate the other. In fact, balanced yin will naturally lead yang. Balanced yang will naturally support yin. How do you personally ascertain whether you are in balance with the yin and yang energy within your physical, mental, emotional, and spiritual being?

Ask yourself: "What are my primary motivations? What are my goals or dreams? What do I personally create by way of my physical existence on Earth?" If the answers are in the nature of competition or seeking of power over others or gaining physical assets, then the yang energy is in an imbalanced state.

People who possess balance in their yin energy will be able to respond easily to these questions. It might be that the responses are vague or dreamy in the sense that you might say that you aspire to a peaceful coexistence or to be abundant enough to have supplies to share with the less fortunate. This is a good start. But yin energy is not merely a meditative or dreamy energy. Balanced yin is strong and active. By following the initial questions with an inventory of what you can actually accomplish, you are engaging the supportive yang energy aspect of the equation. This gives the yin energy a platform on which to take action.

Yin-based answers will include concepts of nurturing and sharing, growing and instruction, and creating and supplying. What will not come to mind in a balanced yin individual is the concept and drive of acquisition at all costs or the separation and control of people. Again, these are representative of unbalanced yang, which is often demonstrated through aggression and the feeling that people need to defend themselves from some threat, mostly imagined.

Yang aggression can be appropriate when there is a real threat of physical danger. What has occurred in recent centuries is a strong addiction to this sense of danger that has perpetuated the cycle of aggressive yang and passive yin. This pattern can be altered now. In many instances, you can see the assertion of yin principles in the face of great resistance by this unbalanced yang pattern.

Changing Your Life

Ask yourself: "Do I feel a sense of aggression at some level? What is causing such a reaction within me despite my desire for spiritual behavior to be prominent in my life?" If you find that you are not in balance or that you feel weak in any way, do not feel guilty or that you have somehow failed. Understand that the world has gone on like this for quite some time, and efforts to shift into an era of peace and love have been unwelcomed by many. But can you see the changes? Are you capable of imaging the world as a peaceful, coexistent global society? This imagining is the basis for balancing the yin first and allowing the yang to begin to take its rightful place as a supportive and guided structure for the yin dreams.

Forgiveness of self is necessary to achieve internal balancing. Facing the reality of who you are allows you to improve and grow. This is appropriate yang action. If seeking peace and balance for the benefit of others is a motivation to change yourself, then your journey to higher vibrational levels is assured. If you are driven by guilt, then understand that this is a form of yang imbalance, and your shift to a higher vibration must wait until such a time as you can accept who you are at this moment and move from that point without having to dip backward to the unalterable past for the energy of guilt to propel you to change.

Spiritual change can happen in what seems to be an instant to those on Earth. It is only when you bring the sense of gravity to your wishes that things slow down. By harkening backward, you attach yourself not only to your own unchangeable past but also to the weight of human history. This is not where you live, and neither is it where you are going. The present moment is the place to seek balance. The future is yours to image reality as you desire. By releasing past attachments, you engage the active nature of yin and yang. Doing this grants opportunity for motion.

There is little in the Universe that sits still and inactive yet grows and brings forth fruit. Stillness can be appropriate for a short time, yet motion and balanced action will bring change and progress. We remind you now that peace is not passive nor is action aggressive.

Peace is an active state of nurturing and growing, being as one with your surroundings—not seeking to dominate or control, but to guide and tend. Seeking peace, therefore, is an action that leads to the creation of peaceful surroundings. Reaction in anger is only a way to feed unbalanced yang.

The expression of joy that we desire occurs naturally when peace is sought and pursued. The state of joy is not dependent on the state of peace, but each aspect is mutually beneficial to the other.

These two qualities—peace and joy—come together as a strong path to the ultimate power of Source, the quality of love. In seeking balance, nothing will propel your quest more quickly and more smoothly than the practice of love.

Many things can and will push against your personal balance, but the action of love, first for yourself and then for others, will connect you to powers and energies greater than can be understood from the perspective of the physical world. Elimination of the illusion of separateness between the physical and spiritual realms represents one of the next great moments in achieving global balance.

Thus, we say that if you desire a greater expression of balance within your life, tend to the energies of yin and yang within yourself. Seek peace, joy, and love in all that you experience.

12
Five Energetic Categories
of Humanity

AS ABOVE, SO BELOW. Life on Earth can be filled with challenges. It can also be full with purpose. Yet many today ask, "What is my purpose? Who am I at my core?" It is often difficult in this day of relentless media imagery and skewed information to know yourself well, or at all. Many messages arrive to your senses seeking to draw your attention, and many promise some form of happiness or fulfillment. Few if any can deliver on that promise in any meaningful way.

The world society was not always like this. In the past, humans were often clearly able to define themselves and the role they played in earthly existence. The society you live in today is an anomaly in the history of humanity. Soon, within the next one hundred years, there will be a strong return to a simpler way of life. Until then, we offer you a path for finding your pure core energy.

In an energetic way, there are five general categories of human beings. Being aware of this can grant you insight into who you are and what your smoothest and most beneficial path through your current incarnation might be.

It is timely to revisit this information we first presented in *Coalescence: The Future of Humanity*. We also offer additional insights as to the current energetic progression of humanity.

We provide this information with the understanding that there are no strict boundaries between these types of humans. These concepts simply represent strengths within you. You might fall into one of these categories quite easily. If you have always been attracted to the qualities of one of these paths, it is an indication of who you are at a fundamental energetic level. If you have not been following that path, it is never too late to begin.

We are often asked whether you can be in more than one of these categories or even switch from one to another. Yes, you can do these things; however, the recommendation we offer is to play to your existing energetic strength within this current incarnation. By trying to fulfill too many different roles, you could dilute the life you are leading and not feel fulfilled as an individual.

If you feel that you are not living your life according to what your strengths are, then this information might help you to see the disconnection of your energy with your current incarnation. It might be that you will change the direction of your life.

The Five Categories of Humans

We will speak of the human beings in each category—the Walkers, the Watchers, the Knowers, the Growers, and the Harvesters—from the perspective of their most balanced existence. Humans often find themselves struggling for balance in today's swiftly shifting society. What we present here is the ideal for each category.

Walkers. These humans are the ones who move about, searching and exploring the world. They are seekers of new paths on the physical plane, new approaches to life and existence. They are often tinkerers and mechanically minded, inventors and discoverers, and innovators of dwelling lifestyles and alternate-energy sources and transportation. These are the members of the family human who most often presage the next great leap forward.

Watchers. These are the humans who keep the flocks and tribes safe, maintaining oversight and supervision. They are often alone and as such may "hear" differently as much as they "see" differently. The bigger picture of the greater good of the tribe is often in front of them, but they are equally interested in the details, the individual humans. These members of the family human are most often concerned with the emotional balance of the tribe and are often the spiritual leaders or directors.

Knowers. These humans gather and collect knowledge, philosophical and scientific, categorizing it into usable forms or locations for others to use. They could be referred to as librarians, but they are not limited to books or recordings in the traditional sense. They also have access to higher realms of thought, but this is not always apparent to them individually. In a balanced world, these members of the family human most often play the greatest role in the leadership of tribes.

Growers. These are the humans who institute new plans and ideas, germinating the concepts and potentials for using raw matter. In a very real way, the Growers tend the seeds and create fertile fields to sow. This goes beyond literal farming. This would include those who design and engineer projects. They are different from the Walkers in that the Growers work with what is already in existence whereas the Walkers discover new things. The Growers are those who bring life into line with the flow of the universal energies. Ones in this category can also be referred to as healers, those who promote health and vitality.

Harvesters. These humans harvest and remove matter once its purpose has changed. This includes those who process and manufacture, crafting items for a future use. In some cases, this includes people who instruct students to achieve higher levels of knowledge and awareness. From a spiritual point of view, they are often those who assist life to advance into the next stage. This, then, includes moving from a current incarnation on Earth to the spirit realm. The purpose of the hospice worker is well defined in this category. Harvesters do not remove life; they only assist one to move from life. The role of the Harvesters is an ever-increasing one. As this world continues, there will be a greater need for these ones to step forward.

The Progression of Humanity

So we present to you the five general energetic paths that a human can follow: the Walkers, the Watchers, the Knowers, the Growers, and the Harvesters. However, these are not simply categories of humanity; they can also be considered stages of human life from conception to the final breath, in much the same way that a human grows through the seven primary chakras. When you are young, newly born, your first chakra is very, very strong. There is very little of the seventh chakra active in a newborn. You see, they have just come from that place of spirit life! As humans age, they go through the second chakra, the third, the fourth, and when they are more mature and have reached a certain age, they return in an older state to that seventh chakra, that place of spiritual connection, when spirituality is more important than mere survival, the things the first chakra is more concerned with.

Humanity as a whole goes through those stages. Currently, humanity as a whole is living through a Grower stage and nearing a Harvester stage. This is where all that has been grown over the past century and a half begins to be harvested and utilized for a greater purpose. All that has occurred in the recent past is going to energetically feed the next century, and then we go into a Walker phase once more. The Walkers are the explorers. They seek, they study, and they bring back knowledge. They will have new territory opening, and they will be given new maps based on all that humanity has experienced. So that is where you have been, where you are going to be, and what will come in the future.

Again, as we have mentioned before, there were energetic limitations put on humanity over the past decade, and it was a difficult growing season. So the Growers are tired. They are discouraged. Many have lost heart, those who are of the Grower energies. The Walkers and the

Watchers, they both have sort of stepped back and are being still. The Knowers are often still. It is the Growers and Harvesters who are now coming to the forefront, and many of the Growers are seeking something to do. There are not enough Harvesters in the field. Some Growers are feeling themselves beginning to shift energetically into Harvesters.

The Growth of the Harvesters

The Harvesters process is changing. They shift and alter vital forces and energies when they are no longer useful in the form they are in.

There will be much transitioning of life from Earth to the realm of spirit in the next decades. This is hard for some to hear, for life is sacred, and that is not wrong, but death is also sacred. The transference of energy at the end of a life, a peaceful transference, allows you to return to heaven, the spiritual realm, in a pure and easy way.

A peaceful transference from the family human to family spirit—how much more pleasant that is than to cling to a weakened life in pain and in suffering and in agony and a false sentimentality? The Growers are now gaining an understanding of this, and seeing the opportunity to participate in what can be considered growth from the planet to the realm of spirit, they have begun to move into support positions with the Harvesters.

Harvesters do not take life. They assist in its transference. They reassure. They comfort. They allow one to relax through the transference. They create an opportunity for a change of mind—a change of thought and emotion regarding what is commonly termed "death."

Look back to those who were of the nation of the plains, the indigenous nations of this North American continent. Understand their wisdom regarding death, their wisdom regarding the animals, and their wisdom regarding themselves and their role on the planet—not as owning the planet, but being owned by the planet. Know how advanced they were in their spirituality, advanced from where much of the family human on the planet is today.

All life falls into these five general categories. It is possible that you could feel drawn to more than one. It is possible that you have felt a shift from one to another, as many have felt the shift from Grower to Harvester. It is advisable, and we remind you now, to follow the strongest path. This will allow your life energies to flow naturally; thus your time spent on Earth will increase in quality.

One category is not better than another. Each has its joys. All who are following their strong energetic paths will soon feel a greater sense of peace about their lives on Earth.

In the end of each incarnation, each human will feel the release of gravity and the entry into the realm of spirit. It is here that all the energies coalesce in a harmony of love. It is from that state of love that we offer you this knowledge. It is in the interests of your hearts that we bring this communication to you.

13

Gaining a Higher Perspective on Your Place in the Universe

AS ABOVE, SO BELOW. As beings in the spiritual realm, we speak from a vibrationally elevated position. The information that we bring is not always wisdom; often it is simply a different perception that we offer. It is not always intended as guidance but rather as a conversation between companions who coexist in two different phases of the Universe.

We remind you of this now to help you better see who you are while in the physical form of a human. From our perception, there is an oddness to human societies. That oddness takes the form of the need for many members of the family human to feel inferior to those who exist in the spiritual realm and thus to feel compelled to grant worship or obeisance. We assure you now that this concept of worshiping spiritual beings as if our perception makes us better is not something that is asked for. It is simply misunderstood. This would be like worshiping someone because that person stands on a mountain and can see further. In truth, anyone can climb the mountain and gain the same perspective.

Those who feel the need to worship something or someone are experiencing the primary imbalance of energy that still affects Earth. This has been the imbalance for nearly twelve thousand years of human existence. It is patterned after the imbalance of energies affecting the planet and the solar system. It did not have to go this way, but it did. Thus, we say it is a system, and it is in place. We do not fault.

From the spiritual realm, we do not fault nor judge what any in the physical realm do. Although there is much in the physical realm that shows the imbalance of energies, it is recognized also as a realm of filtering. You are going to have imbalance and impurities in the physical realm.

You Are Physical and Spiritual Beings

The path for all humanity while on the planet is to seek to behave in a way that balances and purifies the vital forces of Gaia. This requires an elevation of vision away from the individual being and an acknowledgment that there is a greater purpose to life, a purpose that exists in a time far longer than human existence. Yet many believe they, as the individual, are the most important consideration of all. This inflated sense of self perpetuates the imbalance and prevents many from achieving a pleasant relationship with those in the spiritual realm.

Members of the family human who live their lives in this unbalanced state often do not get past the sense that there is some heavenly reward or punishment. They do not quite comprehend the continuity of one's karmic line of energy as not being destroyed but rather existing always as an opportunity for continued growth.

In the physical realm, there are astronomical markers. On Earth, for example, there are days of equal light and dark, called equinoxes. There also are times of the year when there is seemingly an imbalance of light and dark, commonly referred to as solstices. While this is an actuality, it is also a representation of the true path of energy around Earth.

In the physical realm, light and dark are equals. Over the course of time, there is an equal amount of light and darkness on the planet. Even then, darkness is an illusion. It does not mean there is no light; it means there is less light. There is a purpose for less light: a time of quiet, peaceful reinvigoration of the physical form. These markers of shifting light and dark on the planet offer opportunities as reminders of rebalance, reconsideration, and new possibilities.

Because you are born to this planet, the planet possesses you. All of the atomic structure that makes you a physical being comes from this planet. What does not come from the planet is your karmic lineage. What does not come from the planet is the higher vibration encompassing and surrounding this system of planets. The energy of the spiritual realm is difficult to detect, yet it constantly affects the physical realm.

The cycle of karma, a being's karmic lineage, corresponds with astrological and astronomical systems. You have more planets that flow in what can be called an even orbit around the Sun. You also have one that you know of that flows in an uneven elliptic. Karmic lines are affected by that planet as it shepherds energy, reaching out and pulling things back that might be escaping the gravitic energies of the Sun.

The solar system has been chosen as a place of vitality, as a place of growth, and as a place of purification and filtering. As the Sun moves, the Sun pulls the planets behind it. They are attracted to the Sun, so they follow. We remind you now that it is not a simple spinning about the star in flat orbits; it is the spiraling that happens as the planets follow. The universal energies are in a constant spiraling motion.

Sometimes the vitality of the planet, that energy that we seek to balance and purify, can trail and fade. We do not want that lost in the galaxy, we do not want it alone, and we do not want it abandoned. So there are planets beyond the outer orbits, bodies whose gravitation pulls this back into the solar system and cycles it back. This is closely tied to karmic lines. It is what allows some karmic consciousness to exit the planet and be off the planet for long periods, and yet they always get shepherded back. You must understand that this goes on so much longer than simple recorded history on the planet.

We, Onereon, are within this boundary too. We are just at the top of the mountain and can see farther ahead, and farther back as well.

Transitioning to a Peaceful Era

Recently we have all moved from one plane to another plane. What we mean by this is that there is what you might describe as a top and a bottom to the galaxy. So let us say that we have moved from the bottom to the top—

or maybe from the top to the bottom. We have passed the point where the energy has been taut, tight, and restricted. The echo of that energy will continue. From our higher perspective, we can tell you that the energy is loosening, and it was bound very tightly during this passage. It will take a long time for the relaxed effects to be felt fully on Earth.

You, however, will begin to feel the ability to relax, to release intensities that you feel, letting go of guilt or of the need for righteous purpose. We are very careful as we say this. We are not saying to cease living. We are not saying to cease planning or cease directing your energies. Only allow yourselves simple moments of quiet peace where you do not have to feel the need to pursue elusive, fabricated goals. Return to the point of being rather than doing. Be open to putting your house in order. This is a greater energy that is around you—that of putting your house in order. Your efforts in this regard offer consequences appropriate for your future growth, and growth is a process, not an event. So you must release the quest for certainty.

We suggest a more peaceful approach to your life on the planet: not passive, but diligent, step-by-step. Patience will serve you during this time. That recent energy of oppression, constriction—there are still many eddies, many waves of that energy, and waves echo back in a direction against what the tide might be. The incoming tide must interact with waves that flow out again. Things get smoother from here on, on the planet. But smoother than a violent storm that has affected human society still is not smooth sailing. You have weathered many of these storms.

Tend what exists. Help others tend what they have. Be at peace with your situation. The opportunities for growth will approach.

The energy currently on and around the planet is just too unpredictable. It is too vast. We can tell you that obstacles—energetic obstacles—once were thick and only recently have they begun to thin out. The path ahead is clearing. There are unseen things in the galaxy that your solar system is passing through. They have some gravity. Some of them are physical. Most of them are not.

This planet could still experience great difficulties. It is frustrating because we often say that the near future is good, better, and unrecognizable from the past, and that is a true statement, but the path to that future could be one of difficult times. Many alive today will leave this planet before they achieve satisfaction in their lives.

By asking, "What *should* I be doing?" you raise the concept that you might somehow be doing something wrong, creating an internal self-judgment that takes you away from the present moment. There is much to be said about living in the present moment. Joy begins in the present moment. Watch children and observe how they consistently enjoy the present moment. Their joy disappears when they are taken away from the present moment or when someone takes their present moment away from them and puts expectations on them. Exist in the moment, and you will feel joy reveal itself to you.

The generations that are now concluding their passage on Earth have been a bridge. We have said these words before. Despite the societal chaos that seems to be engulfing the planet, there is no need to regret actions taken. They have not wasted time. They have held space. There is no judgment. Despite the potential for continued difficult times, there are joys available in the coming years. Take those joys gratefully. If you are not feeling joy, you must ask yourself the difficult question: Why not? The answer will generally be because there is expectation attached to your thinking. Release the expectation. Embrace the joy.

Release guilt. When you feel the joy, just feel the joy. You know your spiritual path is true when you feel joy. It really is that simple.

See yourself at peace. You are a spiritual being in a physical realm. Your lives are not mistakes or in error. They are one short segment of your karmic cycle. There is no cosmic punishment. Do your best in all things.

Purify all your encounters by coming from a place of love. In this way, peace will flow from you like water from a spring. Do what brings you joy. Live life simply. Allow any false feelings of guilt to flow away. In difficult moments, begin with joy, allow peace to exist, and then love yourself first and foremost.

14
Releasing Burdens

AS ABOVE, SO BELOW. In the realm of spiritual beings, there is a higher perspective—less restriction and fewer (what might be perceived as) boundaries. It is, in many ways, easier in that realm to encompass the concepts of growth and balance and to put into motion the principles of spirituality that many on the planet desire. In comparison, physical life on Earth is, by its very nature, a denser vibrational existence. There is often a sense of struggle to achieve a spiritual life while incarnate.

When things become difficult, humans use the phrase: "Things are getting heavier." Indeed, there is often a physical rearrangement of a human's posture. They bend down, as if there is an actual weight, a burden, that they are carrying. Their heads and their shoulders drop as if bearing a physical weight. When events in life become difficult, in a sense, they are energetically carrying a burden of heavy, thickened vibrations. They feel the energetic weight of their situation.

There is a phrase we are currently hearing from many: "I am so done with *this*." Are you done with *this*? When will you be done with *this*? The reality is you are never done with *this*, meaning the continuum of your karmic existence. But a density has been developing for several decades that is affecting those who are alive on the planet. It is bearing down on humanity as well as other beings in the physical realm. It is wearying. When people say they are "done with *this*," what they are in fact looking for is a shift in the heaviness they have been feeling—some movement and some open doors. It is natural to seek growth and movement. It is a primary principle of the Universe, and we remind you that you are a particle of Source energy.

The Spectrum of Vibrational Existence

As vibrations intensify, they thicken and harden until they eventually become stone. They become solid matter. In the spirit realm, vibrations are farther apart. They are higher, and they consist of energy, not matter. When we speak of vibration, this is the best illustration we can give to you in a sense of how the Universe works. At the physical level, it is difficult for humans to fully comprehend the complex action of the Universe, of the actual matter and energy of the Universe.

The energy of coalescence pulls things together, concretizing certain situations to a point where they do not move easily. The elements that make up the thickening vibration are not easily used again unless that vibration is broken up, in a sense. The illustration of what Earth passed through in the past several decades was a vibrational tightening—a steady intensification of vibration in which very little movement was capable of occurring.

Although there is a loosening, you are not long out of that energy; thus you can expect that energy to echo. That tightness may return to you. This energy is around you on Earth and much of the galaxy spirals through it. It is neither wrong nor right. It just is.

By way of further illustration, imagine a fruit press for grapes or other types of fruit. As the vat filled with fruit is subjected to a crushing stone or some other mechanism, the fruit yields its juices. Once the juice is freed, what remains is a denser matter of pulp. In much the same way, as vibrationally heavier things become concretized, lighter things are able to be squeezed out of the heavier matter. You may not see these light things now. The heavier the vibration, the deeper and denser the vibration creates an opposite and equal reaction. Greater light is squeezed out.

For the world, there are lighter things being squeezed out of this heavy, dense vibration. We remind you, we do not speak only to America. All around the world, these things are happening. Let us talk about the physical planet itself. The actions of the planet are often reactive to other things that are happening elsewhere on the planet. As the substructure of the crust changes, the crust must change, so there is settling that occurs. Do not be overly fearful of this settling. Earth has done this far longer than your scientists imagine.

For most of human history, the species (now considered humans) and their nearest ancestors coexisted with the planet and understood settling action, and in a sense, they honored it and went along with it. In this way, they survived and thrived. They often moved from areas of shifting and what might be considered danger, long before such events occurred. They sensed, as do many animals today, the inherent approaching of instability. Rather than seeking control or continuing in denial of planetary changes and alterations, they cooperated with Gaia and flowed to another area of growth opportunity.

In a sense, that wisdom has been lost in lieu of the pursuits of science. The quest to quantify has limited and, in some cases, eliminated the ability to communicate directly with Gaia. Listening to Earth will bring far better results than quantification, yet you are far from this. Quantification itself is not in error. But it should not become the primary source of information. Gaia's variability and diverse behaviors will not allow for faultless predictions.

The shaking of the ground, the settling, this is just an increase in vibration creating a denser crust in the areas that it affects. Then firm crust can be built upon by Gaia herself. Does this mean more and better land for Gaia's life forms? Yes, it does. Does this mean more and better land for Gaia's life forms in the shape of humans? Not necessarily. It is a mistake to believe that humanity owns Earth.

We are moving toward much more stability on the planet. Yet much has to shake down, to settle. The density of the vibration creating thicker, harder crusts on the planet stabilizes the planet in these areas. It also means higher vibrational energy is squeezed and released from out of the ground. Space occurs. We remind you again that we speak in vibrations, using the vibrational terminology as a simplified illustration of a complex action of constant creative interactions. Planet Earth is a creative energy, and there is much power stored within her physical existence.

Affecting the Physical and the Spiritual Realms

You can witness the increasing movement of Earth's crust through quantifying instruments. Is it any surprise, then, that there is a corresponding shaking of the mental and emotional existence of humanity alive on the planet these days? This too will have a desirable result, but just as the fruit in a crushing vat, the process of attaining what is desired will not leave things unchanged. Enlightened producers know that the remnant pulp is still useful but only when removed from beneath the crushing weight and processed differently.

You have come through heavy times in the past couple of decades, and you will see echoes of those times. You will seem to regress at certain points. It is hard to say "trust" because you are so done with the heaviness. You are weary to the point that even when you are in a good situation, it feels heavy. You are weary to the point that even when you are in a good situation, you find yourself intensifying the heaviness with your complaints, dialog, thoughts, and conversation. This is not a judgment; it is merely an acknowledgment of how easily even higher vibrational beings can slip into lower vibrations.

You know people who are stuck in a heavy vibrational way because they are judging. They are absolutely sure that they are absolutely right and that other people are absolutely wrong. However, from that judgment phase— those absolutes, that heaviness, that denseness, that pressing down—previously restricted light is released. Higher vibrational activity is released. Spiritually observant people look at those heavy judgments and say, "Wait a minute, that situation is *not* absolutely right or wrong," and then they turn away and look for something different, something new. They seek motion and flow and harmonious action with the Universe. They gain perspective. They look for the way that allows for growth, the way that allows for shining, bright light.

In a way, we speak of the fact that there is no judgment in the Universe. There is no right or wrong. There is no heaven or hell. There is merely growth. There is spiritual growth. There is returning to Source. Those who promote judgment and punishment, those concepts, you see, they create duality. In order to create it, they must imagine it, and they imagine themselves in it. They become fearful. Releasing the need to judge is one of the higher, easier, and most basic ways of attaining a spiritual nature. No good and no evil—only consequences for your actions. Just life. Just existence. Just returning to Source. Just raising vibration and lightening up.

Sometimes the vibrational existence of physical life is so thick that even higher vibrational people are caught in the thickness of it all. Sometimes it can seem just too difficult not to judge the situation. The heaviness of certain situations creates a gravity all its own and draws you down. Release judgment of others when possible. If it does not seem possible at the time, try to remember what we say, "Do not waste your words." Do not argue. Do not try to convince. Pull your energies in. Listen to what others say. Do not absorb. Do not agree. Do not disagree. In this manner, you remain neutral. If you find yourself in a situation in which others are judging you but you are neutral, none of these judgments will stick to you in the long run. Also, you will not judge any of the situations around you and thus will not have to find out later on that you were in error, perhaps, in your weighty judgment.

Actions That Assist in Raising Your Vibration

A powerful guiding principle is: "Will this action contribute to growth or inhibit growth?" Notice that sometimes an action will not directly support growth, and a different action will actually inhibit growth. In this case, take the action that will not inhibit, even if growth is not supported. Take the action that leaves things at a level where more action can be taken in the near future.

In the case of potential conflict, do not be afraid to withdraw. Do not be afraid to step back. Neutrality is a form of courage. Courage, we remind you, means to follow your heart. Do the best you can. Be prepared as best you can. Maintain a high spiritual level, the best you can. Keep your heads erect. Keep your chin up. Keep your heart open. Keep your brain engaged.

Do what you need to do. Do not put excess pressure on yourself. This takes away the joy. Seek the joys that you desire in your spiritual pursuits, and speak about those joys to others of similar vibrational nature. Breathe. Physically lean back. Physically stretch your chest and arms to better open your heart until you begin to feel the peace you are seeking. Taking this pose allows the sense of heavy burdens to be released from your shoulders and neck.

The physical toll that this world takes on each one of you disturbs the peace that you can create. The heavy vibrations of this world can be compared to loud, sharp noises. It is difficult to relax under such pressure under such vibrations. It is difficult to love those who create such noise. When you find it difficult to love those others, look to yourself and ask what it is you love about you. If you discover it is a short list, then you know where to begin your work!

It is important to remember that you are an element of Source, and Source is love. Love is the primary energy of Source. If you lack the ability to love yourself completely, do you see how the creative, higher vibrational energy of Source is then limited? Lengthen the list. Love yourself more.

We reiterate the words with which we always close these sessions: "love, joy, and peace." Live in the energy of love and joy. We wish you peace, even though it might be difficult to come by these days. Let it grow. Let peace grow.

15
Moving Forward

As ABOVE, SO BELOW. We often speak of balance. Gaining and maintaining balance is a primary pursuit in a spiritual seeker's life. It is a constant effort in an unbalanced society or when engaged with others who do not share your spiritual inclinations.

For over a decade, we have spoken of the energy around planet Earth as being tightly wound, difficult to move through, and dense and heavy. You have felt this and seen the consistent failure of many things in society. In recent years, we have spoken of the lessening of this taut energy. There is an uncoiling of energy in this area of the galaxy, especially in the solar system we inhabit. You might be sensing opportunity for motion personally. It is still difficult, but possibilities are opening for new potentials.

As a single being on Earth, it requires some level of trust to move forward after such an extensive period of unproductive time. We remind you now of the expression, "Look before you leap," but we also remind you of the concept that you cannot cross a wide gap in two jumps.

Structure is shifting around the globe. The more rigid the structure, the more likely it will break or shatter. There is much that is rigid in current society. The shattering of such monolithic structures may become scary to many humans. Many will seek to shore up the crumbling walls. They will seek to maintain the status quo. What these ones are not seeing is that the world is vastly altered, both on a philosophical level and a spiritual or energetic plane. What appears to many as imminent destruction is in fact simply the natural changes that constantly occur. There is no longer abundant energy to keep old concepts in place. The spiritual seeker will clearly see that placing faith in the past ways of society is not a path to the future. Clinging to the past will only inhibit growth.

The best way forward to the future is to be in motion. What does this mean? Are you to change your address? Are you to abandoned all possessions and live a life of homeless travel? Is there some physical action that will emulate this movement of which we speak? The answer to these questions is simple. The motion we seek is not necessarily a physical movement. It is an energetic motion that comes from your spiritual nature.

We have asked you before, "Who are you now?" We have encouraged a deep self-examination of your current practices and advised a willingness to shift away from old patterns. Even when they are spiritually based concepts and ideas and even when the tenets are rooted in deep guidance and peaceful intention, ask "Is this still truly who I am? Or is this just something I have been doing while the restrictive energies were in force about the globe?"

The motion we recommend is one of energetic shifting to match the new patterns emerging around Earth. Among the new patterns are these general currents:

- the increase and acceptance of diversity in all beings
- the awareness that Gaia, the living planet, is not something that belongs to humanity but rather that humans belong, and will return, to Gaia
- the release of ancient institutions and hierarchies as authority over the family human

As you absorb these words, many of you will say, "That is what I have been saying for a long time!" Others will say, "This is exactly what I want to hear!" It is to these two groups that much of our message is directed today. There is a third group, and we will speak of them in a moment.

For ones who are already aligned to our words, we say, "Thank you." You have been in a difficult place through the years, and you have held space for the energy that is flowing into the world now. You might be weary. You might have been discouraged. It has not always been easy to maintain balance and a strong spiritual nature under the duress of those who seek consistently to take and own the planet or to gain control of the inhabitants. It is hard to walk a true spiritual path when all around you are clinging to old, outmoded religions. You might even have been considered a minority or someone who is on the fringe of the family human. Do you feel the shift now? Is it getting easier to be who you truly are? Again, we in the realm of spirit say thank you for walking the oftentimes difficult path.

For those who we might term newly awakened, welcome! It still is not an easy path. As you learn of new paths available to you, be aware that there could be some who believe their old paths were the best, and they might promote them as truth, expecting you to follow them. This is an echo of old energy. Stay in appreciation of the past, yet move forward in your own way into the future.

The challenges that spiritual seekers still face are similar to what has occurred in the past. There might be mockery or actual verbal assault. In some cases, there could be physical assault. These things can be endured and survived.

The more difficult challenge is the appearance of society seeming to fall backward into an overly yang, unbalanced, aggressive pattern. These illusions and, in some cases, realities can weaken those who have held a strong spiritual space for many years. It is here that the newly awakened beings will be able to carry the elder ones forward by dint of their fresh energy. We are not saying that youth will be caring for the aged. Rather, we are saying that in the current and future mingling of the older generation of spiritual seekers with ones who are bringing new eyes to the concepts of spirituality, there will be a freshening of material, a reinvigorated approach to what feels repetitious or tired to those long-standing practitioners.

There might be ego problems in some of this mingling. All beings who are on true spiritual paths ultimately find themselves challenged by their own perceptions. It is in the releasing of your own judgments that you will make the greatest forward motion on the path to and through enlightenment.

Refreshing the World

As we progress into the near future, you, the true spiritual seeker, will occasionally catch traces of what might be compared to fresh air in a cramped and stuffy room. These moments will be akin to guidance as you search out their origin and move in the direction of that freshness. Give yourself the time needed to search out the path. Do not be discouraged if the sense of freshness fades. Imagine cool breezes arriving on a warm and humid day. They do not necessarily arrive all at once, nor do they immediately cool down the area.

If you are involved in a structured, patterned society that has remained unchanged for many decades or centuries, the sense of freshness might be inhibited, but if you are seeking such an experience, the traces will find you. This is one of the ways that old structures and institutions will collapse. Many seek to feel the fresh energy of the future, and they are willing to make the sacrifices necessary. Without people to prop them up, the old structures wobble and become less important. Soon they are seen to be irrelevant to the evolving world and thus dissipate into memory.

If you have been keeping your own personal nature suppressed for fear of disapproval, these moments of fresh energy will help you see that there is a better way of life than staying hidden from your own true self. Receiving fresh energy will grant you strength to act as you truly are. In pursuing the path of these energies, you will begin to see many who, like yourself, have been in hiding. You are not so unusual, after all! There is more diversity in the world than conformity.

The Universe (and subsequently, Earth) does not support conformity. It does support uniqueness and growth. Allow fresh light access to your true energetic self, and observe how swiftly growth can occur.

This fresh energy is coming from Earth. The changes occurring around the planet can appear to be destructive to some, but the spiritually minded human will be able to take a longer view. It is not simply for one or two generations that Earth shifts and alters. It is in constant motion. Given this idea, you can easily see the value of cooperation with Gaia rather than seeking to prevent her from taking the action she sees fit to make.

The consequences of a mere century of industrial activity by humanity is profound. Gaia, however, has taken larger hits and come out better for the experience.

Seek Gaia's will. Plant flowers for the bees and birds to use for food and shelter. Recirculate water when possible. Minimize use of chemicals when you can. Take notice of the land you live on and act accordingly, not seeking to change your environment to something it is not naturally attuned to. When atop a mountain, do not seek to level the ground. When living in a desert, do not attempt to grow lush grasses. When living in a forest, do not clear large swaths of trees for your personal and temporary benefit. Use the power of the sun and the strength of the wind when possible.

Embracing Change

Here is the key to understanding the future of spiritual practice: Embrace the concept of change. Look for paths that take you into new and different areas, not simply a geographic or physical action, but intellectually and emotionally. Learn new concepts. Explore new approaches to life. Learn to grow something. Write a story. Learn a new creative activity, even if you have never attempted such a practice before. Look at what you believe you cannot do and seek a way to challenge this aspect of your beliefs. Do not put yourself in unnecessary danger, but leave your ego behind and take a risk. These activities do not need to be noble nor have great purpose. They are simple things that you attempt for your own personal growth. Even if you seemingly fail at the attempt, you can say that you tried. In truth, you succeed at expanding your energetic signature on Earth.

Change is the normal nature of the Universe, and Earth is no exception. You belong to Earth and thus are an integral aspect of Earth's changing nature. Any attempt to remain "just as you are" will result in your own creative energy becoming stagnated and eventually blocked. It is only through embracing the energy of change that you, and subsequently Earth and the solar system, will be capable of shifting fully away from past imbalances.

Energy is now being released from the stagnation of the past three centuries. This is not a promise that the changes and shifts will be easy. There may be some swift alterations. The family human is adaptable and will carry on into the future. If you are participating in this activity, you will have an easier time in the next few decades.

This brings us to our third group, those who seek returning to old, solidified energy. They do not wish for change and act in opposition even to the thought of a future variant from the past. They seek to hold together old institutions, to retain ancient prejudices, and attempt to exercise dominion over Earth and her children. They will shout loudly. They will say frightening things and threaten dire consequences of moving away from the past. In some cases, they will attempt to dominate free people. In others, they will use technology to bring their invasive thoughts to the forefront of human consciousness. It could even seem that there is a powerful surge of support for such an energy. We tell you now that it is an empty sound. It might echo for a brief moment, but the outcome is that eventually it will fade and lose its source energy.

Earth—Gaia herself—will continue to shift and change, and the vibration around the globe will continue to rise. As it does, the family human will respond to the rising and purifying energies that are finding fertile areas to take root. Ancient, restrictive thought will not be able to trap or imprison you if you are in motion.

Supporting the Shifting Energy

The future is growth and motion. Not every seed becomes a successful plant or tree. Yet each seed provides a lesson. The physical matter of a plant goes back to the soil and enriches Earth whether the seedling becomes a tree or not. Eventually, even the tallest trees and the strongest plants and vines will find themselves cycled back into the earth for Gaia to use their energy once again in a new and diverse way, as will all life on Earth.

This is not fatalistic. It is realistic. Embracing this concept frees a spiritual seeker from the need to "be something" or gain notoriety. The long view of life is not attached to the short span of human life. Rather, the cycle of life is the long view, and this is a true spiritual point of meditation.

As the world continues to alter and shift, we will all begin to see clearly how patterns of the past will conclude and new, fresh patterns will emerge. The energy is clarifying around the planet and through the solar system. A time of change has begun, and many have preceded you in the work of spiritual nature. These ones have passed from Earth now and, if you choose to believe this, you will understand that they are now in an altered form, a spiritual form. Only, like a tree that comes from a seed, they are being offered the opportunity to also become seedlings once again. You will receive this same opportunity when you leave the realm of gravity.

If you are a human incarnate upon the planet today, you are primarily of the earth. If you feel an affinity to beings from the stars, this is a clarifying vision, and one that you will more accurately understand when you exist at a different place in the cycle of life. Ponder such things occasionally, but you have volunteered to be here on Earth now, so keep your attention more directly on Earth and the important work offered to you here. From another point in the galaxy, you are doing cosmic activity!

Seek motion, and consider that motion to be spiral in nature. Image spiraling streams of power within you. Image the patterns of force and energy flow as spirals in the palms of your hands and other strong chakra points. This will empower you in difficult times. More than that, it will channel strength from the Earth and increase the vibrational aspect of Gaia's presence in human lives.

We have passed a specific point in the space-time continuum. There is no going backward. The future is one of great change and balance. Some of you will see sweeping changes firsthand from a life on Earth. Others will cycle through, perhaps several times, until the completion of the shift.

We tell you now that the future is the one you have been seeking. It is an image that you have carried forward from the past and continue to create. You have been strong in holding this image in place.

Now we ask that you speak of the world as you imagine it. Speak of a time of peaceful coexistence with the planet. Sing, write, paint, or otherwise create joyful images of things that make life here on Earth so unique and beautiful.

The most challenging thing of all is to remember to act in love when you encounter those who seek to hold you back. Do the loving thing always, even when it's difficult. Better days are near. You are the example for the generations arriving now. Welcome them. They arrive in gratitude to you for your great spiritual actions.

16
Out of Chaos and Into Peace

AS ABOVE, SO BELOW. Those who are spiritually minded human beings often question things. These people tend to see deeper into the course of the world. They notice many things that others accept without question or apparent thought.

Their questioning takes the form of observations: If there is increased enlightenment on the Earth today, why is there so much trouble in the world? If we are nearing a better, more peaceful future, why does it seem that wars and violence are increasing? What actions are correct? What paths should a spiritually minded being take to help the world gain that which appears most humans desire?

The Near Future

We often speak of an impending golden age. This is a true thing, and it is happening sooner than an individual human may be capable of believing when observing the chaotic world you currently exist in.

First, there will be a time of increased conflict. Everywhere on the globe there will be challenges to what was once considered order. There are leaders and would-be leaders who speak as if they alone possess the absolute truth about matters. There are people who appear to be following blindly, illogically, in the wake of some who seem determined simply to create rough waves. The waters are muddied and the currents confused.

Still, there is greater purpose to all this confusion. The past was a world of inequality. The societies that held sway for many centuries were imbalanced and aggressive. These monolithic entities of government, banking, and religion will not easily shift their paths or accept that they are outmoded. They will seek to maintain their dominance over the populations of Earth.

The energy for such behavior is now altered and continues a course of change. There is no longer power enough to prop up such structures. That energy is being redistributed around the planet. People are seeing the results of archaic and obsolete philosophies instantaneously, and those same people want something better, something more equitable.

The humans in existence on the planet today sense the will of Gaia at a more powerful level than at any time in the past three thousand years. Gaia seeks balance, and her human stewards are awakening to this call.

This will take some time. There are beings who are weak in their ability to discern what is a balancing action. They are often easily led into believing that unbalanced activity will restore the world to a mythical peace of the recent past. We remind you now: there has been very little peace available to human societies around the globe in the past three thousand years.

Discernment and Self-Balance

What distinguishes those who seek balance from those who seek to maintain old, patriarchal, imbalanced yang dominance? The words being used are key to understanding the thoughts. You must first listen to the words one speaks, but then you must take the next step and test those words. Is there truth being spoken or have the speakers merely said what the people in front of them want to hear? Exercising discernment is paramount to each individual. By separating what is false in a speaker's words, you take steps toward creating balance. This does not mean you must personally challenge falsehoods. Rather, you should take the action necessary to draw energy to balance. You might disagree with certain people, but by engaging in dialogue, argument, or any attempt to draw their followers to your own path, you become imbalanced yourself, as yang begins to grow inside of your own karmic entity creating a desire for dominance over another.

There is a phrase used, and within this simple sentence is much wisdom: "I will not dignify that statement with an answer." An imbalanced statement needs no reply. By seeking to explain, you offer energetic support to a statement and supply it with power. Let the falsehood and imbalance falter, fall, and fade naturally. In this way, you maintain an internal harmony and outward balance away from the chaos created by argumentative beings who seek to gather power to themselves.

What does an imbalanced being speak about? First, imagine what the will of Gaia would be, or ask yourself, "What does Gaia desire?" Then compare those responses you intuit with the actions that certain domineering humans engage in.

Gaia seeks to have harmony amongst the various ecosystems. For example, this does not mean all animals live in peace with one another. Rather, it means that there is a strong, sustainable food supply for all beings. We do not say only all sentient beings but rather *all* beings that exist in and around Earth. Gaia seeks to have her systems honored and to be allowed to function as designed.

Gaia's ecosystems are continually shifting. There is variance and growth always. In that growth, there is often erosion and seeming destruction of land or plant life. A closer examination shows that felled trees decay and provide places of growth and nourishment for smaller seeds and insects that reseed the forests. Water washing away stone creates new, clean silt and soil for perpetuating growth along rivers and creeks. In the cycle of life and death, humans and other mammals make room for new beings to be born and to enjoy life on Earth. Harmony does not mean perfection. It means balanced existence.

Gaia is not physically smooth and regular. She is not prone to creating artificial boundaries or borders. She does not prevent one ethnic group from traveling about, nor does Gaia seek to build walls of separation. Her rivers and mountains can appear to be barriers, but this is only one way of viewing such natural formations. It is a limited way of envisioning the beauty offered.

Humans have been gifted opportunity to create craft that allow for travel on waterways, both great and small. Humans have been given inner strength to climb and explore mountains and other areas seemingly inhospitable in search of secrets of the works of Gaia and the galaxy. The purpose of a human life is often one of gaining knowledge and sharing such knowledge to create a greater wisdom for the human race. A human who seeks to control or censor accumulated knowledge is not one who acts in the interests of Gaia or humanity's future.

Areas of geography affect humanity differently. People from varied places around the globe are energetically different from one another. It is this diversity that Gaia seeks and offers humanity as a path to a peaceful future. Embracing cultural differences shows the sign of a questing and accepting energy, a growth-oriented being.

Balancing Behavior

Building walls and enacting restrictive laws does not speak of acceptance or love. It might give the illusion of peace, but there is no joyfulness associated with such fear-based actions. The illusion of peace gained is one of isolation and a feeling of superiority over others.

True peace is accepting and curious. True peace pursues and spreads the joy of life. Together this peace and joy cultivate love. Love of life comes first, and when enough people around you are feeling a true love of life, this allows the freedom of self-love to flow within all humanity. This is the future we approach. We gain this soon through the chaos that is the erosion of the old rock-like communities of imbalanced power bases.

There will be uncertainty. There will be angry rhetoric. Observe these things, and comment on them, but do not seek to engage and create arguments for or against any harsh or extreme positions.

The essence of a spiritual being is found in the words and qualities that best reflect Gaia's pursuit of balance. In this, then, if you choose to follow a spiritual path, seek peace and joy. Act always in love. Support those who are strong in seeking balance among people all around the globe.

17
Karmic Reality

As ABOVE, SO BELOW. When we, Onereon, express this concept of "as above, so below," we are cognizant of the mental disconnection felt by most of the family human. To contemplate this—the continuation of your life while not incarnate on Earth—is difficult for many. A primary reason for this difficulty is that there is so much misinformation and so little reality of perception when humanity searches for answers regarding the continuum of life after their short spans of consciousness on Earth.

We have spoken of karmic energy and karmic generations. In addition, we have used the term "karmic thread" when referring to a continuity of life before, during, and after an incarnation. Let us delve a little deeper with the understanding that it is not easy to comprehend the full reality of karma while in the lower vibrational state of earthly life.

Release Dualistic Concepts

First, karmic energy is not to be understood in terms of punishment and reward. This is a mistaken interpretation brought on by fear-based, dualistic beliefs. We acknowledge and ask that you become aware of the fact that within societies known to history, there are often groups of people who have a vested interest in promoting the theory of cosmic punishment and reward. We are stating this only as an observation of imbalance.

Karma is not, as is commonly misunderstood, a system of judgment. It is more the idea of consequences or consequential action. The sum of one's deeds and decisions constitute their karma. In this view, the path one chooses is a personal creation of karma rather than being at the mercy of some higher power. This is the seat of the concept of free will. Some feel that they are blessed while others feel cursed by circumstances of birth and life. Karma, understood as a path of free will, allows all people to shift and alter their paths.

The energy of karma, while affecting you personally, is not isolated. Each being in existence on Earth feeds the energy of karma. Each being interacts energetically with others and often choices that we make individually are influenced by considering others' potential reactions. This includes not only sentient beings but also all things that possess even a rudimentary consciousness. Animals, birds, even insects might create opportunities for you to create a karmic action. And each action taken by another being creates a potential opposite and equal reaction in you. By fully exercising your awareness and spiritual consciousness through your free will, you can create a better and more balanced moment of time.

These balanced moments of time, then, become higher vibrational points of brighter light, purer energy, and points of guidance for other beings. These moments do not have to be great decisions or discoveries. Indeed, they are often simple, some might even say mundane, moments—for example, when you choose to accept a situation rather than become angry or annoyed. In the examination of karmic activity on Earth, it is often what one chooses not to do that is the greater aspect of raising one's vibration.

Weaving a Strong Karmic Web

Karmic action is a complex web of energies. Consciousness regarding this web of interconnectedness leads to a higher vibration on the part of an individual. If one acts in a balanced manner, balanced life will become more natural and common. Likewise, when people act in an imbalanced manner, their incarnations can (and often do) spiral into lower vibrational existence. When dealing with imbalance in societies, it is easy to get caught in a cycle of reaction or to allow consciousness and spiritual awareness to become sublimated.

There is a broader and more subtle energy throughout the Universe. In this area of the galaxy, you on the physical Earth and those of us in the spiritual realm who remain close to you are isolated somewhat from the broader karmic actions of more distant beings. This allows for some measure of freedom to accomplish a purer balancing around the solar system. This also allows for a delicate individualism, a personality, that can be identified and maintained beyond the physical world.

In other areas of the Universe, the energy of an individual consciousness often merges with the greater energy of higher consciousness. In those areas, there is less separation of life into smaller and individual events of perception and experience. Here, in our local system, we can possess a strong sense of personal continuity and, if we are strong enough, become a karmic entity that maintains a line of remembered perceptions and patterns whether in the physical world or in the spiritual realm. This is why some are capable of recalling what are perceived as past lives. The reality of such past-life recall is that if you have strong enough energy, you can pluck such recall from the broader web of karmic experience. However, it is easier to gain clear recall when the majority of your energy participated in those past events.

When a strong karmic entity again becomes an incarnate human, the amount of retained energy that makes up such a strong entity is vaster than can be contained within the physical form of a human life. An aspect of this karmic entity then becomes the "above," or higher consciousness, companioned to the "below," or lower vibrational being, experiencing events of physical reality.

When one is possessed of great awareness or infused with a high level of purified, balanced energy, this being often becomes a strong spiritual being, what is often termed a master. That term can carry judgment within its meaning. It can imply that such a one is somehow higher, more powerful, or deserving of reverence and service. True masters know that their paths are not that of being served or revered. Rather, their paths are of being of service to others. The term "Bodhisattva" clearly conveys this description. A strong karmic entity connected by clear awareness of the karmic web serves to create greater opportunity for increased karmic balance in the time and place that they live.

There have been many such ones, but often their messages are subverted into dualism and false belief of an absolute right and an evil wrong. No Bodhisattva has ever taught such a thing. They see the karmic web that all beings weave together by their actions, both here on Earth and also when they exist in the realm of spirit.

The Unique System of Karmic Generations

The karmic web woven with the threads of a karmic entity's continuum of lives is sensitive to and creatively responsive with the energies of the space-time in which they currently exist. Maintaining karmic continuity will grant a steadier progress of purification of energy. Within this continuity exists a type of karmic wave action or what we have termed karmic generations. Here is where we, you in the physical and we in the spiritual, in this section of the galaxy are unique amongst much of the known Universe.

Around the system in which we exist, there is an observable pattern of those who return to Earth together and those who also depart under certain circumstances. The currently active karmic generations, of which you are a part, are a culmination of a great diversification of energy deemed necessary to accomplish a specific task, balancing a strong presence of unbalanced yang energy that arrived in our section of the galaxy in what is referred to as prehistory.

The society that existed and was lost to that unbalanced energy was powerful and well balanced with Gaia. We, in the spirit realm, could have deflected such energy from Earth, but then it would have continued on to some other area to have an unknown effect. The choice, and some of those who are incarnate today on Earth were amongst the choosers, became one of acceptance. We gathered ourselves together to share a unique event.

It has taken tens of thousands of years to achieve the point of life we now enjoy. The balancing and purification is ongoing, but much has occurred in recent decades that now opens up a clearer path for increased peace and harmony to once again exist amongst all of Gaia's life forms.

There are many who, in their higher consciousness, see great changes and shifts approaching Earth. In their human consciousness, having been affected by the imbalanced yang for so many earthly genetic generations, they misinterpret the massive alterations of society as destruction and judgment. Nothing could be further from the karmic reality.

In the current day and age, you observe two things happening: The first is rejection of continued judgment based on outmoded and illogical philosophies. The second is a strong fear-based call to cling to such ancient misinterpretations of spiritual principles and is a final burst of the energy of dualism. It is a fading system that will no longer easily work under the newer karmic awareness and successful efforts of the current and near-future karmic generations.

This new karmic awareness allows for the higher concepts of love and joy to not simply occur at special moments but also to grow and flourish in all activities that a human might engage in while alive and fully present.

Enhanced connection to one's higher self is really a clear perception of the karmic energy that binds us all together in a larger and purer holistic system.

This is the way of Source. This is the way we feel the true expression of Source energy, the energy of active peace, conscious joy, and unqualified love.

18
Karmic Generations
and the Future

AS ABOVE, SO BELOW. We offer these words as a beginning. They indicate that we, in the realm of spirit, are not so different from you alive in the present day on the planet Earth. Yet humanity will often approach the ones they refer to as angels and guides with questions or requests. It is an ancient arrangement that has run its course. We, above, are now dealing with you, below, more or less as equals. There is a growing maturity level in spiritual seekers of the physical realm that allows for greater companionship and clarity of communication. It is the culmination of many ages of separateness and the beginning of a new way for life around the solar system. Still, the realm of spirit beings is here to continue guidance while we pass into this newer age.

Often we are asked to speak on the topic of the future. Many have a desire to know the outcome of their work here on Earth. Will life become better? Will the world improve? Were all the studying, training, learning, and service to others really of value to humanity and to Earth? Is the new age real or only a dream, wishful thinking?

In almost equal measure, we are questioned about the elements of the past. Where did humanity actually come from? Is the history we are taught true? Is there some hidden gnosis that we should be searching for, an ancient library awaiting discovery? Then there are those who seek some assurance that the present day, troubled and strife ridden though it may seem, will carry some greater meaning, that all we are going through will somehow be significant and valuable.

We can tell you clearly, the past is not as you may have been taught, the future is brighter than you can imagine, and the present day is crucial and pivotal in the continuum of life in and around the planet Earth.

The Generation of the Present Day

There is a generation departing Earth and another now arriving. These two generations have been and will be the most influential beings to have existed on Earth in all recorded history. It is not that they altered society completely, though they did; rather, it is more the strength and growth they individually revealed as incarnate karmic beings to accomplish this task. And it was a task, a purposeful decision made at a higher vibrational realm. The outcome was not a predestined thing. Chaos and reduction of life may have occurred and was predicted by many seers in the distant past. Those seers adhered to strict and structured dualistic philosophies of absolute goods and evils. These belief systems clearly represented and illustrated the imbalanced yin and yang around Earth. There is still a strong remnant of such destructive philosophies remaining.

There is a third generation we will talk about—the current generation, the ones who are maturing physically and beginning their lives and careers and families in the midst of all the confused energy that exists today. They too have a task to accomplish. They too are strong karmic entities, but their strength is different. They are durable. They are improvisers. They are survivors in a way that cannot be imagined by the departing generation and will only be fully understood by the arriving generations.

The End of an Energetic Winter

Consider this illustration: Imagine that autumn turned to winter early. Imagine further that the winter was the stormiest on record. Many lived at the edge of the sea, and a mighty river emptied into this great body of water. Miles away from the large population on the sea was a smaller, new settlement, pioneers who were seeking to establish their own paths and lives.

The winter winds and weather patterns gathered the cold air and swept it about, chilling and freezing everything exposed. In the larger city, there was still trade and supplies from the great sea. Life was difficult, but the buildings were strong, and established services kept everyone supplied, minimizing the risks of winter.

However, in the newer settlement up the river, supplies ran low, and the waterway became completely frozen over. The ice expanded to depths never before recorded. In order to get supplies to the community, the frozen rivers became paths, but the fierceness of the temperatures and blasts of wind prevented long travel. They were left to fend for themselves.

The arrival of spring was welcomed, but there was much damage, and pioneering settlers were weakened. The river began thawing, but could not be walked on any longer, and it was still iced over and could not be sailed. A group of people from the city by the sea created an icebreaker, and they took to the river in an attempt to open up lanes for sailing vessels. It was difficult and perilous work. Often the icebreakers got stuck in the river and were not easily moved. Slowly, the weather warmed, and the ice became easier to break and separate. The river was still treacherous, but there was more and more open water. Others began to risk their smaller vessels and navigate the icy waters. Loss occurred. People perished in the tasks they accepted.

The warmer weather continued to melt the ice, and those settlers farther up river began to see hope arriving in the form of battered ships and watercraft delivering desperately needed and gratefully received food and fuel from the established society by the sea. It seemed life might actually return to something comfortable. Growth once again seemed possible.

Well into summer, large blocks of ice continued to be spotted floating in the river. But what was once necessary to break up became only necessary to be observed as it floated away to sea to melt and no longer be dangerous.

People could see newer ships arriving that were clean and undamaged. They were piloted by many who heard of the terrible winter but did not experience it firsthand. There was respect given to the survivors, but the people in the new ships left to get on with life. Their purpose was not to listen to the stories of the past; they looked ahead to their future.

So it is with the world and the societies of Earth now. The pioneering ones who were lost and frozen are the middle generation of beings in the present day. The icebreakers are the generation who broke apart the old stuck energies and are now preparing to depart Earth. Those who deliver fresh supplies are the ones who are new to Earth, recently born to the planet and beginning to practice new ways. The new ones bring hope to the survivors of the harsh winter.

Pondering Our Place in Time

The past is important. When there is time to spend in contemplation, it is enjoyable to ponder and meditate on what went on before. But there is little in such musings that adds to the present day and the abilities necessary for spiritual growth. The future will arrive soon enough. The most interesting thing we can tell you about the future is that in some form or another, you, the spiritual seeker, will see it firsthand! It might be that you are incarnate once again on the planet, or it could be that you will see things from above, in the realm of spirit. There is not something written that can be revealed in detail. It is, however, a future shaped by those who are of the generation now departing Earth.

There is no specific timetable that we refer to in this discussion. Many alive now are of that generation that we refer to as departing. Never fear, we are not predicting a catastrophe that ends with multitudes passing. We simply refer to the natural cycle of birth and death. The term "generation" is a broad one when referencing life on Earth. It is different when we speak of a karmic generation, and this is more of what we are seeing—three distinct groups, each with its own path and vision and each shaped by the events that preceded its life on Earth but each determined not to repeat the patterns that came before.

A constant thread in each of these karmic generations is the betterment of life for everyone and everything here on Earth. This, then, is the primary difference between the three groups and all humanity of the past two thousand years or more.

Together they share a vision of what is possible, a vision of peaceful coexistence with all of Gaia's life force. They seek to promote love and harmony within every community, ending strife and the destructive nation-building efforts of ancient dualistic philosophies. They strive to gain the most enjoyment from their time on Earth, releasing minor annoyances in the hope of creating a large and joyful community of beings from all walks of life and all areas of the globe.

Are you seeking such a future? Are you acting as if it is already here in the present day? Open your hearts to truly see the hope that is being offered to the society of the family human by spiritual seekers from both above and below.

19
The Future of Prophecy

AS ABOVE, SO BELOW. It is said that the only constant is change. It is accurate to make this observation. You can add to the depth of this truth by realizing there is nothing that remains the same. All existence is a flow of energy that moves in spirals and waves on all vibrational levels. Even that which appears still to the observing human is altering and shifting at subatomic levels, at energetic levels that you are incapable of witnessing.

Yet you are on the path to greater awareness of higher vibrations. Your sense of reality is altering. Your understanding of yourself and the Universe is coalescing. There is no goal, only flow.

Allow the consciousness of your current existence to release any perceived need to understand or leave a legacy and your sight and vision will instantly increase.

You are in motion. You are a travelling energetic being amidst a vast oceanic flow of energy. You are a particle of Source and the Universe. What Source experiences and observes can be accessed to a lesser extent by humanity. You can "see" the space-time continuum, but you cannot fully comprehend what you witness.

Comprehending Vast Energies

We all, together as denizens of this solar system, pass through the Universe, and most of the humans that have ever existed did not even realize that such travel was happening. They believed that Earth was a stable place and sought, and often fought, to maintain the illusion of consistency. Most of the family human live life unaware of the magnitude of existence, accepting that what they see with their immediate physical sight is the only reality that needs to be recognized. In truth, the multitudinous layers of energy that coalesce to make just the single planet of Earth are miniscule compared to the immense forces and combinations of power that emanate from the central Source of all things.

We all possess a sense of the vastness, and when we are in a lessened physical state or when we relax and open to a meditative moment, the greater energies can be sensed, if not completely comprehended. It is not unlike observing the surface of a wide river or deep pool. There can be eddies and currents observed, moments when the water whirls in a spiral, but that which is deep cannot be seen. Even if we immerse ourselves into the body of water, we become subject to its actions and force. We are able to observe small areas and, in so doing, seek to interpret and collate our minuscule information into a larger truth. Yet the higher meaning and understanding of where the source of such a body of water begins and where the water ultimately flows to cannot be divined from such limited experience.

We are all curious beings, and inherent within us while incarnate on the planet is the strong desire to understand, connect, and gather information that allows a higher perspective to enhance our lives. In the daily routine, we find ourselves grounded in lower vibrational activity. Only when we take time to be still and quiet do our minds begin to sense what is often called a reconnection to the spiritual realms. This is what occurs in meditation or prayer. We are connecting at a very limited level with power and force so far beyond our ability to comprehend that there is no way for us to give an absolute truth to what we observe. We are compelled to try to connect the observation with what we know. In this way, errors of perception occur. Assigning names and genders to life forms that exist at higher levels—or even attempting to explain the higher vibrational levels of existence themselves—is destined to be an erroneous interpretation of a vision.

The primary source of all difficulties in human society these days is an insistence on the correctness of an interpretation and a coercion of others to a specific way of belief. This is true of religions, certainly, but also of social systems, political ideologies, and economic structures. The solution is not as simple as eliminating all belief systems in an effort to resolve conflicts and difficulties. These patterns of belief are deeply ingrained in most of humanity. There is power and flow to this old and ancient way. Those with a strong desire to maintain stability and retain personal power over others find comfort in a level of certainty and the philosophy of "knowing your place" in society. Such a way eliminates the need to strive for something better. Acceptance becomes a comforting veil.

Now we see a change in humanity. There is a willingness to leave behind many of the old images and systems of belief. It is a shift that is inherent in the area of space-time that we are travelling through in the Universe.

A purifying, balancing energy will clear the path for greater connection to the creative energies of Source. This is not to say that there is a smooth transition in process— quite the opposite. There first needs to be a fuller realization that realities not yet beheld have already occurred and have gone unnoticed by the vast majority alive today. A prophecy of global change has long been held, but few understand that this reality is and has been upon them for decades now. They do not recognize it as such because they choose to believe a preconceived notion. However, the truth of something becomes like a rising tide, and soon there will be no way for any human to ignore the shift that has already occurred.

Remnants of a Misunderstood Vision

Let us pause a moment and discuss an old vision. For many centuries, we saw humans, primarily male, who allowed themselves to delve deep into their consciousnesses. In so doing, they witnessed a parallel existence, a greater existence beyond what they could fully comprehend. The purpose of many of these men was to establish a form of power and structure for their own benefit or that of an immediate leader. Seeking to validate an existing opinion is never a path to truth. They did not take the time to expand in consciousness to comprehend the depth of their visions and realize a greater, more harmonious time was arriving.

What they witnessed, the gift they were given and wasted, was a vision of the potential future. In their imbalanced state of seeking control and power for themselves, they interpreted the vision according to what they understood: the lower vibration of conflict, destruction, plagues, and general misfortune leading to scenes of vast death. This became a primary prophecy. It led human society far away from the principles of spiritual growth and harmony with the rest of creation. Those men failed humanity by turning the vision into a vision of failure.

You can see that the misinterpretation of this vision led humanity away from that which they sought, a close relationship with a loving god. The result has been a further separation of most of humanity from the creative energies of Source. We note now that the vision was not an error, only the interpretation. What was viewed as destruction is in fact vast change. You are in the midst of that change now.

The same energy they observed is now the energy that we—in the solar system, certainly, but also in our vast, star-filled arm of the galaxy—are passing through now. It is not an energy that can be observed at the moment by scientific instrumentation. This is only because humanity does not readily see what it does not know to exist. Only in the deeper states of consciousness are you capable of observing these galactic currents and eddies. Even then, you will be unable to correctly interpret the meaning. This is not a fault. It is what it is. The experience of not knowing is valuable to the greater experience of the karmic entity.

Those who seek to prophesy the future with exactitude will find themselves to be unstable in their answers. A prophet must be cautious not to be self-serving but also careful in the feelings and emotions they instill. If the stated interpretation includes fear and destruction, the listener must ask themselves, "How often have I heard such a prophecy of woe? How true have they proven to be? Is there another way of looking at things? Can words and images of destruction be interpreted also as concepts of realignment and restructuring to balance and harmony? Can I live my life differently and remain in joy despite the anger that exists in others?" These questions will assist in seeing the world and history in a clearer light.

Those who look with true spiritual eyes will observe clearly that there are great potentials ahead. They will also observe that fear-based activities are currently on the rise. They could feel fear too. There is fear in the world, and there is reason for such a reaction. Fear is a byproduct of uncertainty and instability. It is understandable, then, that many would take comfort in the concept of things remaining the same, even under oppression, division, or other imbalances. This is not why humanity has been given consciousness. This is not why humanity has been gifted a powerful connection to creative Source energy.

What Everyone Dreams

This is the prophecy for the coming times: Humanity is increasingly maturing and developing and is capable of a new way of seeing the old information. The level of spirituality is higher, and the potential for manifesting dreams of harmony and balance are gaining power. You have a role in this, a state of active creation. There is a way of change in process that is more powerful than in times past. It is a path that will offer a greater spiritual world. It is a process. You will see ancient religions dissipate. You will see societies coalesce into something greater but also retain and grow in diversity. You will see areas of Earth open up once again to animals that have currently diminished populations.

The quality of the family human will rise but not without a great shift. There will be a reduction in the quantity of humanity but not necessarily due to great cataclysm. Cataclysms will occur, and this is due in part to human actions. Much, however, is cyclical, and once again, we remind you of the galactic energy of change that we pass through in the Universe at this time. The vision of a violent apocalypse is passing away. Few believe it any longer, but those who do are shouting louder than ever before. They too will pass, and the energy of their belief will diminish and dwindle as humanity achieves a new balance.

It will not be perfect. Nations will continue, and divisions will occur. What is occurring now is the final tightening of an overabundance of yang energy. If allowed to continue, there will be a destructive explosion of power. This power, like all energy, is ultimately creative, though often the prelude to creation is chaos and a reduction of existing structure.

You are and will continue to see such a dismantling in your present day. The destroying of old systems and outdated rigid rules is occurring at a rapid pace. Sometimes it might seem that the old ways are returning or that they are too strongly entrenched in the fabric of consciousness to ever be swept away from Earth society. Yet it is exactly this entrenchment that marks the inevitability of their alteration and shift into something new and different.

Soon there will be an active period of time that could, on the surface, appear to be a kind of doom for earthly society. Pay attention! All will not be as it seems.

What will eventually grow is a fuller comprehension of the holistic nature of the solar system and thus the galaxy. The implication is that the universal energies will come into fuller view, but this knowledge is far off, and there is no certainty for humans in this form. Connection to Source through creative and meditative activities will offer glimpses now of these vast powers and potentials. Be cautious with what you observe. Be responsible with what you say to others about your personal visions.

The flow of creative energy will be further recognized and revealed as loving and peaceful. This is the true meaning of the term "apocalypse," a revealing of what is true, a lifting of an obscuring veil. In the recognition of this power will be the return to fuller connection of Source and humanity. In this return to creative energy, we will see the end of talk of and images of destruction and the action of death dealing. The shift in perspective will occur, and the culture of fear will fade. Balanced creative energy dwells on growth and nurturing all life.

The future will be a time of allowing the energetic flow we have spoken of here. It will be humanity living a life of clarity and harmony that has no direct need for visions of the future. The present moment will be full with comfort and satisfying activity. The concept of prophetic visions will cease to have the meaning of "predicting the future" because all beings will possess access to the flow of energetic observation. Humanity will sense a fuller connectedness to the Source energies that we exist in and will flow along in the ocean of space-time. The veil of complacency will vanish like a dissipating fog, releasing all life to a certain clarity and surety of the continuum of existence.

Prophetic messages that contain the concepts of peaceful coexistence, the images of joyful lives of abundance and health, and the powerful, unifying force of love amongst all beings will bring the greatest clarity of spiritual vision to Earth now and intensified into the future. In this way, prophecy predicts an end to the need for prophesying.

20

A Challenging Path
to a Better World

AS ABOVE, SO BELOW. We are often asked what the future will bring. Within this question is the seed of hope but also the germ of despair. In asking, humans want to know that their efforts are not being wasted and that their lives matter. There is a seeking of validation, a pursuit of feeling that there is hope for the future and that perhaps some measure of balance and peace might be experienced in the current days.

The Perils of Prediction

As Onereon, an entity of communication and service, we do not claim nor offer prediction as a matter of course. We do, however, possess the ability to notice things from a higher perspective. What we see are not often specific events but rather trends and currents.

Things we see do not easily quantify into a specific timeline. The future is malleable and can alter based on unexpected events. The reality, as we currently perceive it, is that the future is divergent and can take two paths. Both paths will arrive at a similar destination. One is easier than the other. The approach to life and living that will always lead to growth and abundance is the yin path. This is nurturing and nourishing for all beings involved. The future holds an abundance of yin energy, but we are not there yet.

The past has seen an extreme imbalance of yang energy. We must point out that yang, in and of itself, is not "bad" or "negative" energy. Out of balance—that is, when yin is suppressed—yang often becomes aggressive and seeks to dominate and rule rather than govern and lead.

You can see clearly in the passage of recent history how yang has been out of balance. For over two thousand years, human societies have increasingly been subjugated to this domineering approach. During the past three hundred years, we have seen a destabilization of this imbalanced yang. This is marked by a return to people-centered governance and less religious rulership. Increasing democratization of cultures and fuller emphasis on personal spiritual connection is the yin path.

However, the imbalanced yang does not yield easily.

What Can Be Done Today?

Each human is an aspect of the creative energy of the Universe. In this realization, we see that we can manifest realities into our lives through imaging techniques, meditation, or prayer. There are a great many powerful beings on Earth today. There is also a growing strength to the yin energies available to human societies.

The future of a peaceful and growth-oriented human society is, while not exactly a foregone conclusion, highly probable. By spending specific moments imagining what elements that might include, humanity alive today sets in motion the yin energy to a fuller and faster realization of such an outcome.

Yet you are each faced with steep challenges to believing this reality is possible. There is a very real effort to subjugate the majority of the population of Earth. There is a very real effort underway to weaken resolve and hope. This energy seeks to distract from what is truth or philosophically yin oriented. This is not simply a matter of differing perceptions. There will always be that aspect of life. This is a matter of seeking to regain or retain power over others. It is the last bit of strength that the imbalanced yang has gathered in an effort to remain dominant on Earth.

You can see this clearly throughout the world. It requires that you become a critical thinker, exercising logic often, especially when you hear news reports or view fabricated biased events. There is war being waged in various portions of the world, and this is not being reported clearly. There are great humanitarian disasters occurring, and aid is being hindered. The environment is teetering on the brink of collapse, much of which was once preventable but now is closer to inevitable on certain parts of Earth. There are unbalanced mass attacks on innocents based on unresolved and misdirected personal anger. Each of these elements requires those responsible for the imbalanced action to narrow their viewpoints to the exclusion of reason and love. Each of these elements represents a failure of imbalanced yang to act in a responsible manner toward Gaia. This failure of imbalanced yang will ultimately bring about the change that many seek.

Will we find it necessary to go through great disasters to gain the balanced world we seek? Here is where the path ahead is divergent. Here is where we, as spiritual beings in the spiritual realm, can offer a higher perspective and speak cleanly about the future.

Much depends on what the majority of earthlings manifest in the next ten years. Already, we can see that the times will be difficult in many ways, but only if you try to maintain old patterns. Those who seek to cooperate with the natural patterns of the planet will find that they are free of many of the deep concerns others are going to face. Again, what you image in your heart and brain will prepare your individual energetic being for this coming time of planetary change.

Accurately Envisioning the Future

Once there were a great many visions of cataclysm and what was referred to as apocalyptic activity. A broad shift in humanity's spiritual nature allowed for that eventuality to be sublimated and eased. In other words, the so-called end of the world was cancelled. We are not now suggesting that the potential for this action has returned. We are saying that if the majority of humans choose to image destructive things, then the chances are greater for that to occur.

To avoid this scenario completely, it will be necessary for every human to shift his or her mental and emotional patterns to peaceful and loving thoughts. This will not happen. There is too much residual fear available to too many humans. What can be done, however, is the many who sit passively—content in the belief that nothing needs to be done and that somehow spiritual beings will handle all the work—must take action. It is not enough to merely believe. It is necessary to act as if the world is already in that peaceful and loving space.

It is a correct assumption that spiritual beings will handle most of the work. The point here is that humans are those spiritual beings who will do the work. There is no difference between those you call angels or spirit guides and yourselves except that you exist incarnate in the physical realm. In fact, you as a human have much of the same ability as we in the spiritual realm possess. You can and do create what are often known as miracles. Does Earth need some miracles these days? You, as a spiritually minded individual, can enhance the process of miracles!

This, then, is what we bring to you regarding the future. In a short time, there will be increased evidence that humans can and do create reality. Many who have had difficulty with this concept will be given reasons for belief. There are many who wish this to be true, but they doubt. Fear has affected their hearts. Soon many will understand the true nature of creative energy. It will begin within the next few years.

Balance will not be achieved soon, but steps toward increasing balance will be visible. There is still much that remains of the old patterns. Look to new religious leaders to overturn those old archaic structures and release judgment. Look to new governmental leaders to stand up and speak out about the imbalances remaining. New ideas are being prepared. New patterns are being established. It will take another two generations for them to get a steady motion, but there is much that can be accomplished in the world today and in the near future.

Act in thoughtful ways. Do not engage in conflict, as this supports and gives energy to aggressive yang. Engage in discussions in which there can be multiple perceptions, but do not insist on any absolute conclusion. Every human is different, having had wide-ranging experiences. You will not all agree on every point. Debate is natural and yin-oriented. Argument is a way of seeking dominance over others and forcing them to a path not their own.

Search for ways to help others—humans and animals certainly—but also Earth. Reduce what will remain after you have left the planet. Think of the next five generations, and prepare the planet for them.

The ability of humans to seek a vision of the far future is unique amongst life forms upon the planet. It demonstrates a higher vibration, one not shared by the so-called lower orders of animals. Note: this does not lessen the role that animals will play in shaping the future.

The action of visualization requires a being to be willing to behave in a manner that serves others, those who have yet to be born. It demonstrates a willingness to express the quality of love despite the fact that there is no specific being in existence to receive that love.

Seeking to create a future of peace is a calling of far higher vibration than merely seeking to create a better life for yourself. It is a long-range effort in which the person attempting to manifest such a peaceful time must understand that they themselves will not be witness to it, at least not in their current incarnation. This, then, requires self-sacrifice of time and material.

Acting in joy during the present difficult days is a matter of faith in many ways, and it is an expression of confidence as well. A balanced human will seek all these paths—those of love, joy, and peace—as they join one another in this vision of future days of peace and harmony.

21
This Is a Test

As ABOVE, SO BELOW. Many are asking: "With all the spiritual awareness growing in the world, why is there not more positive energy available to current society? Why is there such increased friction and division even between people who are united by so many desires and hopes? Why does anyone seek to destroy others who are innocent? Why is there such discord and anger in the world when it seems as if so many desire peace and harmony?"

The answer might not please you. Many of you are spiritually minded seekers. You offer grateful thoughts and send love and light out into the world when disasters or tragedies occur. You meditate and pray. You seek to live consciously, manifesting peace and harmony. But we ask you, is that enough? Or is there more that can be accomplished? What is the real reason for such deep discord on the planet now?

Many plead with those they view as their guides or angels to intercede, to grant individual requests for personal peace and balance. And answers often do not arrive to their complete satisfaction, for the world never really shifts. Or so it seems. Is it possible that the real reason for such lack of harmony is purposeful? Is there something that you should be doing differently on a personal level?

As beings from the realm of spiritual existence, we see and often are able to adjust the course of energy by affecting vibrational patterns. But this ability is not omnipotence. It is, rather, a setting of example for life that exists on Earth to learn from and act on. In small ways, it can seem like prayers and petitions are being answered, but the truth is that the more powerful your connection to Source energy, the more often you answer your own prayers.

We in the spirit realm simply exist in what is conveniently referred to as a higher vibrational realm. Humans can achieve a higher vibrational existence also, and it is those who seek such a spiritual life that hear us with deep comprehension now through these words. Again, the answer you seek might not be to your immediate liking. It is, nevertheless, a truth.

The Effect of Lower Vibrations

We are, in a very real sense, lowering the vibration of the planet. Deep, booming noises, sharp bursts of emotion (especially anger), bright flashes of light being emitted from a multitude of now common sources, uncommon and unnatural smells, and bitter acidic tastes in necessary water and other fluids are slowly creeping into what is called normal human experience. It is like the illustration of a frog in boiling water. If you boil the water and then drop the frog in, he will jump out immediately. If you put the frog in the water at a cool temperature and slowly bring it to a boil, the frog will remain complacent until it cooks to death.

Other examples of this lowering of vibration include the sharp divide between radical expression of opinion and the cooler, logical approach to life. Note how we do not say "radical thought processes," for there is little about balanced, active thinking that can be extreme. The brain is largely a rational muscle primarily acting on facts and physical principles. We witness the heart as the apparent source for radical reaction. It is the heart disconnected from the brain. The heart is most affected when the vibrations of existence become lower.

When you hear loud percussive music, it can assault your chest and heart area in a way that a physical blow cannot. Your bones, specifically the ribcage, act as a shock absorber in protecting the area around the physical heart. This is, according to ancient understandings, the space where the so-called heart chakra exists. It is the central core of the human energetic system and where your spiritual balance grows from. Interrupt the heart energy by pulsing loud, percussive music or concussive sound effects, such as explosions or prolonged screaming or yelling, and you disturb not only a being's spiritual balance but also his or her ability to remain connected with Source spiritual energy. Even intensive dialog or ranting can have a cumulative effect that permeates the physical body and disrupts the natural, peaceful rhythms of the heart chakra.

Why, then, are we saying that we, in the spiritual realm, are purposely lowering the vibration of the planet? Understand this has been done before, oftentimes over large-scale periods, generational or longer. In a sense, taking this action now is the straightest path to breaking down and removing powerfully entrenched energetic blocks.

We often speak of the coming new age or golden era. We tell you that we see an approaching time when there will be a harmonious series of human generations on the planet Earth. This, from our perspective, will stretch not just decades but rather centuries and has the potential to last far beyond that. However, lessons will be learned before this age fully takes root, and you are living in this time of lessons. With lessons come tests. The lowering of vibrational energy, thus allowing humans to be, in a sense, distanced from Source is that test. As an individual, you must remain in a spiritual state to pass into the newer energetic reality. It will be difficult.

The Narrow Path to Higher Vibrational Existence

Your generations, those of you alive today, are a bridging energy from old ways of aggressive yang and passive yin into a new path of balance. Again, that balance must begin with you as an individual, an undivided one. Only then, when you have possession of your balance and can reach Source spiritual energy on your own, will your vibration be fully raised to what might be called a strong, pure note. When there are enough humans emitting this pure note, the lowered vibrations will begin to rise. This must come from Earth. This is not a process that can be accomplished from above, in the spirit realm.

That the yang imbalance is a wider scale action than solely on Earth is true, but Earth and all of Gaia's life forces have been chosen as a filter and space for this balancing process to occur. The weight that you feel, the heaviness of the lowered vibrations, is (in a sense) acting as a press, squeezing out that which is valuable and vital and leaving the dregs to be recycled and repurposed.

There is no foregone conclusion to any part of this process. The prophecy we offer of a golden age is truth, and it will arrive. It can be here sooner or later. The more humans that take a higher vibrational path, the sooner this age can occur. Taking a higher vibrational path is not to say that all beings must be in some religious or political agreement. It is to say that whatever differences any group of humans has with another, each is capable of finding a way to peacefully communicate—that is, commune, with one another.

The concepts that arise with higher vibrational awareness include strengthening all beings, not just humans; assuring supply of essentials to all beings, not just humans; and concern for the rights of others for a peaceful existence, no matter who or what they are or believe, including beings that are not human. We make the strong point regarding beings other than humanity because a great point that tips Gaia's life force off balance is the erroneous concept that humanity is superior to Earth and other life, that it is somehow a pinnacle of evolution or creation.

There is some truth in the perception that the family human acts in a higher capacity than all other life, but the inherent misunderstanding in those who have been taking a path of power over others is forgetting that humans are meant to act as stewards to Earth and all life—not dominate life, but secure a coexistent path. There is much scientific progress in this way, but it is not always readily available to all life forms. There is much philosophical understanding of basic rights, but it is often subverted for mere profit. The ones who seek and acquire that profit do it solely for their own lifespan and that of their immediate heirs.

There is little benevolence involved in the actions of so many wealthy humans, and the wealth often does not last in a single family for more than a few generations. In the meantime, much is wasted, and the greater core of all life, not just human communities, suffers from this greed and the stopping and storing of energy for no truly useful purpose. Wealth is a form of abundance, but true abundance is shared wealth.

Spiritual seekers sense it. You feel the pivot point.

You are aware of the moments of destiny occurring: the rising incidents of single human violence against mass groups, the fierce and unreasonable rhetoric of the super-rich, the insistence that such rhetoric is logic, and the lowering of the crowds' vibration through simple, mindless slogans chanted again and again—not just political, but also religious slogans and aphorisms.

Repetition of archaic and meaningless ritualistic verbiage in those who do not seek reason from within their own balanced minds—that is, their brains and hearts acting in concert—or in those willing to follow rather than discover their own paths of balance, allow them to abdicate their thinking abilities and react to primal, animal nature, in many cases, lower even than animalistic behavior.

The Test of Life

You are being tested. It must be this way at this time. You ask about the pain and suffering of the world. Can it be that you can supply a measure of peace? Or do you feel weakened, cut off from energy? Can you regain your connection with spiritual strength? Have you willingly tested the world and your opportunities to act in a personally balanced way, or do you isolate yourself and refuse to look or take responsibility or to make a measured response to the world around you?

Peace begins in one place: within the undivided human. It is there that the sense of joy also awakens, deep in the area of the chest often called the heart chakra. This joy compels a positive outlook and refuses judgment. This peace from within is power and strength when coupled with the determination to be joyful. In the human, there is a core energy of love, that unconditional state where no matter what danger is occurring you do not seek to judge but rather seek to act in stewardship for all Gaia's life force.

There is a cycle of life. Creatures live, and then they die, but their energy continues. In the physical realm, it is often in the form of returning precious matter to the earth—the floor of the forest or the fields. In some cases, it is that the matter of a being is used as food to sustain other life. Do not judge. Beings arrive in life, and then they depart from life.

It is the human, primarily, that returns in a more conscious state, and it is those humans who act in a higher vibrational way that return in a more complete state. Other beings, beyond humanity, are being raised in vibration, and many of you reading this now understand this, but not all beings are worthy of grand gestures of rescue. Better to focus your energies now on ones who have the potential to achieve their balance. And how best to do so?

Act in love, act in peace, and act in a joyful manner. When you seek your own balance through these primary qualities, the ripple will spread to other life forms in ways you cannot witness while incarnate on Earth.

You are being tested, true. You have been given the appropriate lessons. You possess the answers within. Seek your spiritual core, your karmic memory. Live.

Other books by Jeff Michaels include:

Harmonic Coalescence: The Future of Humanity

Touch the Earth: A Path to Ascension

Beings: A Journey to Joy

Light: The Reason for Existence

Becomes Us All: Visions of Death and Life

Please visit www.OnereonChannels.com
for current information